CHOOSE

LIFE TO THE FULLEST

90 DAYS TO THINKING
AND LIVING GREAT
PART 2

BECCA GUNYON, MCC

WESTBOW
PRESS®
A DIVISION OF THOMAS NELSON
& ZONDERVAN

WestBow Press books may be ordered through booksellers or by contacting:

WestBow Press
A Division of Thomas Nelson & Zondervan
1663 Liberty Drive
Bloomington, IN 47403
www.westbowpress.com
1 (866) 928-1240

Because of the dynamic nature of the Internet, any web addresses or links contained in this book may have changed since publication and may no longer be valid. The views expressed in this work are solely those of the author and do not necessarily reflect the views of the publisher, and the publisher hereby disclaims any responsibility for them.

Any people depicted in stock imagery provided by Getty Images are models, and such images are being used for illustrative purposes only. Certain stock imagery © Getty Images.

ISBN: 978-1-9736-9254-6 (sc)
ISBN: 978-1-9736-9255-3 (e)

Print information available on the last page.

WestBow Press rev. date: 05/29/2020

PURPOSE

"The secret conversations you hold in the privacy of your own mind are shaping your destiny, little by little. With every thought that races through your mind, you are continually reinventing yourself and your future. Research indicates that the average person thinks approximately fifty thousand thoughts per day. This is either good or bad news because every thought moves you either toward your God-given potential or away from it. No thoughts are neutral."

— *Tommy Newberry (The 4:8 Principle)*

If you read Choose Life to the Fullest (Book 1) and started a habit of daily thinking great and inviting Jesus in, this book will continue your routine. It is my hope that this book helps you discover life to the fullest. *"For as he thinks within himself, so he is."* *(Proverbs 23:7 NASB)*

Choosing life to the fullest is about waking up and thinking great, inviting Jesus into our day, and finding ourselves in His identity. Amazing, repetitive thoughts are key to this process.

My passion in writing this compilation started with thinking about my own teenage thoughts and how they affected my journey. Which led to wondering what my own kids and the teens that I work with would read?

What is the purpose of Choose Life to the Fullest books?

After studying authors much wiser than myself, I found that when we wake up and think five great thoughts our brain starts changing. These five great thoughts super-charge our brain. The opposite is true when we wake up and think five self-defeating thoughts, we start the day behind. We are not victim to our thoughts, we get to choose them. As Christians, when we invite Jesus into this process, amazing life-change happens!

Dedicated to my five kids-each of you are a gift

Thank yous:

Thankful to Lexie Fish for editing
Thankful to Owin Gunyon for editing from a teen's perspective
Thankful to Addi Gunyon for designing all the Instagram posts @ chooselifetothefullest
Thankful to Westbow Publishing for being so wonderful to work with
Thankful to Travis Fish for designing the cover

Thankful to my husband, Dan, who encourages me to write everyday
Thankful for my son, Owin, who edits my books and encourages me to live my dreams
Thankful for my daughter, Addi, who creates beauty and speaks Jesus back to me
Thankful to my son, Eben, who thanks me daily for being me
Thankful to my son, John E, who flatters me with his funny compliments
Thankful to my son, Anden, who asks me if I have thought good thoughts today
Thankful to all the teenagers that previewed and gave their opinion
Thankful to my family, our circle of closeness is a blessing- (Jim and Danise Owings, Josh and Meredith Owings, Matt and Abi Tuiasosopo, Micah Owings, JonMark Owings and all my sweet nephews)
Thankful to my Gwinnett Church Family and my Transit Team/family.

ENDORSEMENTS

"Becca and her husband Dan have been a vital part of our church for years now. They have sharpened us with their wisdom, care and love. Much of how they do this is by teaching us how to think. As Becca points out, the choice to live life to the fullest is exactly that — a choice. And it starts with our minds. I believe the next 90 days will shape and elevate your thoughts. When this happens, with the help of Jesus, our lives elevate as well."

- *Jeff Henderson- Author of Know What You're FOR*

"There is nothing worth fighting for more than the faith of the next generation. After spending years in student ministry, I came to the conclusion that there has never been a more challenging time to grow up than now. Countless things compete daily for our attention and slowly cause us to drift from the things that matter most. I have known Becca and her family for decades and have always respected their commitment to the next generation. Paul told us that we can be transformed by the renewal of our minds. I believe this book help us to see what it looks like to practically tap into the power that Paul was talking about. This is a great resource that will strengthen your entire family."

- *Grant Partrick Passion City Church/Location Pastor // Cumberland*

"Proverbs says, 'As a person thinks, so they are.' Hmmm... When Dr. Caroline Leaf says we have to "process over 50,000 thoughts each day and 80% are negative". How do we learn to combat negative thinking, our diminished value to society, and build self-worth? Choose Life provides a framework daily to reinforce thankfulness, plant seeds of hope, offer and allow positive to shed light on shadows of doubt, and provide an Anchor for the Soul. Providing this resource in a time when it's hard to combat the noise to define who we are, who to serve, what's our purpose, and rejoice in whatever circumstances we may be in, is so much needed. Like a tall, cool drink of cold water on a hot summer day. Thank you for faithfully sharing and encouraging us to think different and become different by Choosing Life at its fullest."

- Jim Owings founder of Lord's Way Ministries

ENDORSEMENTS AFTER READING CHOOSE LIFE TO THE FULLEST –BOOK 1

"As we coach and care for the teenagers in our lives, not much is more important than encouraging them to practice renewing their minds. Becca's focus on spending a few moments each day to reflect on God's truth and focus on gratitude is a life changing practice not only for the young people who will build this habit, but also for the parents who're praying them through these tough years. I'm so excited for her to share these insights with a generation of kids who are hungry for them!"

– *Natalie Kitchen / North Point Leadership*
Experience Program Residency Director

"Becca invites you to choose Life to the Fullest by waking up and thinking great thoughts again, and again. I could not recommend this book highly enough!"

– *Lexie Fish (Worship Leader and Project Manager*
of Gwinnett Church Transit/student ministry)

"As a parent, I believe it is life changing and something I will have to instill in my life and my children's lives. The concept of Living Life to the Fullest is a continuous process that we need to be reminded of often. As a teacher, I Love this book and the message it is trying to get across to students. Too many people do not know how to live/experience life to the fullest. It is a lifelong process and skill! Without God, we are nothing!"

– Dr. Natalie Gibson (teacher, mother, leader in student ministry)

"Becca helped me learn to see myself through God's eyes and not others or my own. Her gentle kindness and servant spirit for God shine through her daily as she pours her life and heart into others more than herself. This book is God's heart through her pen expressing the aspiration she has for all people, that they journey to a daily relationship with God, learning to love themselves, the way that God loves them and in turn live their to the fullest.

– Josh Owings/CEO Owings Enterprises LLC,
Ga. State Director US Elite Baseball

"God's heart for us all shines so beautifully through the words found in each devotional. Becca has humbly submitted her spirit, soul and body to declaring Gods truths in a simple, concise and easy to understand manner. The words cut through the chaos and distractions of life to refocus our minds, souls and spirits according to our true identity in Christ. Each devotional redirects our minds away from the lies of the enemy and this world back towards the truth which can only come from right believing and a personal relationship with Jesus. I'm blessed to be ministered to by such a courageous, faithful servant of God."

– Zenda Griebenow,
(Director and Tennis Coach- Zen Tennis)

WORDS FROM STUDENTS (THEIR WORDS, THEIR AGE, AND SOMETHING THEY ENJOY)

"Choose Life to the Fullest has changed the way I think throughout the day. Every time I start to get down or think negative thoughts I remember to change them and focus on what's good. I have been 100% happier and I enjoy life more after reading and applying this book."

- *Owin/age 17/Baseball*

"I believe that our thoughts effect the way we live our life. Sometimes it is difficult to change our negative thoughts and think positive. Choose Life to the Fullest is very encouraging and includes amazing advice for changing your thoughts."

- *Addi/ 16/ Basketball*

"Having struggled through difficult feelings such as heartbreak, depression, and anxiety myself, this book reminded me that God has given us the ability to *choose* an abundant life, despite the hardships we face. I was reminded that feelings are not always truth, and feelings do *not* control us! Through reading this, I was encouraged to stand up to lies in practical ways."

- *Madison/College Student*

"These daily devotions have impacted me emotionally and mentally. Whenever I feel like nothing can go my way. I think of the phrases and topics of the devotions and God always helps me power through it. All it takes is 5 minutes every day and I feel like a stronger person after."

- *Derek /age 16/baseball*

"The 5 questions are the beginning of the devos help me to focus. Sometimes when I read the Bible, my mind will wander, but this not the case with Choose Life to the Fullest. It helps me to actively align myself with what God will teach me that day. I face a lot at school and this may be the only positive word I receive all day."

- *JP/ age 16/ baseball and crossfit*

"I like them because they are short, powerful, and straight to the point. I get distracted and sleepy if people go on and on."

- *Toler/age 13/crossfit and cross country*

"This devotional book is really making me think about Choosing Joy."

- *August /age 11/reading Harry Potter*

"I never thought about a lot of these questions."

- *Pierce/age 10/baseball*

"This is a fantastic devotional. I love the interaction for the daily question (What are 3 or 5 things?) It really made me think. It really helped me focus on casting aside fears and focusing on God?"

- *Emily/age13/loves riding horses*

"This devotional starts my day off with positivity and the right attitude. It reminds me daily of God's love for me and the people He has blessed me with."

-*Ivan /age 16/basketball*

"Choose Life to the Fullest provides truthful and encouraging reminders that start my day off with positivity and help me to focus on what is good. This devotional reminds me constantly of Gods love for me and the many blessings that He has placed in my life."

- *Claire/16/Volleyball and Basketball*

"Mom, I woke up this morning and started thinking of 5 things I was thankful for."

- *Eben /age 14/tennis*

"Life to the fullest has not just made an impact on the way I view myself, it has made a pivotal turn in my relationships with others. We can often start our day off on the wrong foot, but these daily devotionals have made a positive start to every day."

- *Savannah/age 18/spending time outdoors*

"This devotion really helped me see the many blessings I have been given throughout my life. It really helped me to see life in a more positive aspect. I would highly recommend this to anyone wanting a positive outlook on life."

- *Julia/17*

"The 5 questions at the beginning of the lesson each day is what impacts me most, because it puts my focus on God and helps my day go better."

- *Christopher/14/basketball*

"I read this book every night and it brings joy into my life. This also helps me think of all my blessings from God. I am on my second time through because it is so good."

- *Samuel Benjamin/12/baseball*

"Choose Life to the Fullest" is perfect for anybody struggling with enjoying their life in any season they are in right now. Every single day this devotional gives you a reminder of being thankful for your life and choosing joy. This book has changed the way I look at each of my days and instead of stressing about each new day, I am always looking forward to seeing what God has planned for me."

- *Katelyn/18/ loves fashion*

"Choose: Life to the Fullest is a great way for me to start my day! Meditating on God's word through these amazing devotions have helped me live a better, more Godly life."

- *Taylor/age 13/loves dancing*

What am I looking forward to:

1. Having a sleepover
2. Playing with all fam
3.
4.
5.

"It's in Christ that we find out who we are and what we are living for."
(Ephesians 1:11 MSG)

Questions help us. Living thinking great involves asking ourselves questions. Questions are not always fun, because they reveal the truth. Yet, asking ourselves questions and spending time reflecting on our answers can create change. If you have five minutes this morning or later today you can ask yourself:

- What am I thinking about most of the time?
- Do these thoughts make me better?
- Do these thoughts help me enjoy life?
- Do my own thoughts about me keep me down?

Life is so busy—most of us don't slow down to ask ourselves questions that lead to life change. Our thoughts need to encourage us to become our best self. If our thoughts are constantly beating us down, we will live discouraged. So let's change those thoughts! We can like ourselves, because God likes us. Even though we feel like we have flaws, He calls us a masterpiece. Living in the realization that we are treasured by the heart of God leads to thinking better.

Jesus, I invite YOU into my thoughts. Show me all the repetitive thoughts that discourage me. I give them to You. May I see myself through Your eyes. In Your name

What am I thankful for:

1.
2.
3.
4.
5.

What do I worry about?

Most of us have a repetitive worry. Whether we realize it or not—this one thing that we worry about circulates in our mind. The thing I find myself worrying about is something I know God can do, I just don't know *how* He is going to do it, *when* He is going to fix it, and what I need to do about it in the meantime. You might worry about your future, which college you are going to. You might worry about your career, whether or not you will reach your dreams. You might worry about whether people like you, your relationships, friendships. You might worry about something you can't seem to overcome. Worry can turn into anxiety.

Anxiety steals our joy and hope.

This is the advice God offers: *"Don't fret or worry. Instead of worrying, PRAY. Let petitions and praises shape your worries into prayers, letting God know your concerns. Before you know it, a sense of God's wholeness, everything coming together for good, will come and settle you down. It's wonderful what happens when Christ displaces worry at the center of your life."* (Philippians 4:6-7 MSB)

Worry can be alleviated by giving God one worry at a time, over and over again. Every time the worry pops in our head, we can give it to God.

God, I worry about _____. I have a habit of worrying about this one thing (or multiple things). I give it to You, please give me Your peace instead. Help me to trust Your heart for me. In Jesus name

DAY 3

What is GREAT in my life?

1.
2.
3.
4.
5.

"...I ask—ask the God of our Master, Jesus Christ, the God of glory—to make you intelligent and discerning in knowing him personally. (Ephesians 1:16 MSG)

This verse states that we can know God personally. Knowing someone "personally" does not mean we just know *about* them, but we really *know* them. When we know someone, we feel more comfortable around them. When we can ask God to help us understand Him—He makes Himself known. A growing relationship with God is a result of choosing to spend time with Him, some people call this a devotion or quiet time. It is a simple daily habit.

- We can invite Jesus into our devotion time.
- We can thank God for 5 great things, which reminds us of His goodness.
- We can read a Bible verse like the one above.
- Think about how that verse applies to our lives. Writing this down helps.
- Then we can say or journal (write a prayer) about our concerns, struggles, needs, dreams, etc.
- Be still (even for one minute) and ask God what He is trying to show us.

During this time, if we think of something that contradicts the Bible, it is not from God.

Throughout the day, we can whisper quick prayers to Him, just like we talk to a friend.

God, I want to know You in a more personal way. I invite You into every part of my day. In Jesus name

Good things in my life:

1.
2.
3.
4.
5.

"...I ask—ask the God of our Master, Jesus Christ, the God of glory—to make you intelligent and discerning in knowing him personally, your eyes focused and clear so that you can see exactly what it is he is calling you to do." (Ephesians 1:16 MSG)

If you have eyesight like mine, you might wake up to everything being blurry. Nothing is clear until I put my glasses on, or contacts in. When everything is blurry in life, we can't figure out the next step, and sometimes we don't know which way to go. This can be so frustrating! However, when we are growing in our friendship with Jesus—life becomes more clear. When we focus on His words that promise us GREAT things—we can SEE what He is calling us to do. We can take this verse and understand so much about the heart of Jesus, for He stated, *"I came so they can have real and eternal life, more and better life than they ever dreamed of." (John 10:10 MSG)*

What am I focused on?

Is it helping me?

God, I want to clearly see Your heart for me. Show me what You have for me today. In Jesus name

What is GREAT in my life?

1.
2.
3.
4.
5.

"What shall we say about such wonderful things as these? If God is for us, who can ever be against us?" (Romans 8:31 NLT)

I am reading a book by author and pastor Jeff Henderson, "Know What You Are FOR," it's awesome! In chapter 9, Jeff writes about designing a "FOR culture" by using this pattern: "believe abundantly, appreciate consistently, develop intentionally, listen actively, live repeatedly."

These principles apply to all of us in our various stages of life. I have been asking myself in relationships do I: "believe abundantly, appreciate consistently, develop intentionally, listen actively, and live repeatedly?"

You can ask yourself these same questions about your relationships (at home, at work, at school, on your team). The answers are insightful and motivating. If you want to be FOR the people you are around, I encourage you to pick up a copy of this book.

God is FOR us and following His example we can be FOR the world around us.

God, help me to soak in Your love, so that I can be FOR others. In Jesus name

DAY 6

What am I thankful for:

1.
2.
3.
4.
5.

"...I am with you always, even to the end of the age." (Mathew 28:20 NLT)

This is Jesus talking. He is always with us, for we are not alone.

Kind of like air, we don't really notice it, but it is all around us and it fills our lungs. Whether we notice God or not—He is always with us. He is with us every moment at school, in the car, at practice, at work, at home, when we wake up and when we go to sleep. We don't have to figure out life by ourselves. Life is much more enjoyable when we whisper a prayer throughout the day asking Him to help us, empower us, fill us with His love, kindness, hope and strength.

Have you ever thought about God being present every moment like the air we breathe?

God, I invite You into my moments—my thoughts, my actions, my feelings, my friendships, my dreams, my struggles...In Jesus name

When I wake up, what is my first thought? If this thought is not good, I can immediately change it to think, "what are five great things in my life?"

1.
2.
3.
4.
5.

"...If you wake me each morning with the sound of your loving voice, I'll go to sleep each night trusting in you." (Psalms 143:7-8 MSG)

Our thoughts don't control us, our brain needs to be reminded of this. We can wake up and think, " I am so tired, I am dreading (blank), it will be such a long day..." OR our first thought can be, "today is going to be great, God has greatness for me." The first few minutes of our day can determine how we will feel for the rest of the day. We can choose. The conversation we have in our mind can be the encouragement we need to be the best in every area. In addition, if our first thoughts turn into a conversation with God—whether we realize it or not—we are inviting Him to do the day with us.

How does thinking great in the morning become a habit? We can put a sticky note on our phone or alarm clock to remind us when we see it in the morning. We can write a quote or verse on our mirror. We can choose to make each day great regardless of our circumstances.

God, please remind me to whisper a prayer to You immediately after I wake up and help me to identify any thoughts that are not life giving. In Jesus name

I am thankful for:

1.
2.
3.
4.
5.

"Look at me. I (Jesus) stand at the door. I knock. If you hear me call and open the door, I'll come right in and sit down to supper with you. Conquerors will sit alongside me at the head table, just as I, having conquered, took the place of honor at the side of my Father. That's my gift to the conquerors!" (Revelation 3:20 MSG)

Jesus wants to do life with us. He is continually knocking on the door of our life. He wants to be invited into our thoughts, our relationships, our moments, our struggles, our dreams, our memories (good and bad), our longings.

Our simple prayer, "Jesus, I invite You into _____ (my heart, my thoughts, my dreams, etc.). This prayer does something beyond comprehension. When we invite the God of the Universe to do life moment by moment with us, He makes us conquerors. This life is not meant to be done without Him. He knows we need Him and yet He loves us enough to wait for our invitation. By inviting Him in we find what we are searching for.

Jesus, thank You for knocking on the door of my life and caring about every aspect of my life. I invite You in to do life with me. Help me to think what You think about me. In Jesus name

DAY 9

What is good in my life?

1.
2.
3.
4.
5.

"I tell you, love your enemies, Help and give without expecting a return. You'll never—I promise—regret it. Live out this God-created identity the way our Father lives toward us." (Luke 6:35-36 MSG)

Most of us do not have "enemies." However, there are always going to be people we do not enjoy. They are difficult to get along with and, for whatever reason, just bother us. What if we started seeing them through the lens that God uses? When He looks at us, He sees the big picture. He sees our real reactions and what is behind them: our hurt, our thoughts, our insecurities... Usually the people who are most difficult to love or give to are hurting or have hurts that they live out in their actions. When someone hurts us, it often has nothing to do with us, but stems from their own pain.

So what if we lived out our "God created identity" by being so full of God's love that it spilled out on those people who are hard to get along with. Doing this will create a better quality of life for us and for them.

Is there anyone in my life that it is difficult to reach out to? If I look deeper, can I see their pain?

God, help me to see myself and others through Your lens of love. Give me more of Your love when I don't feel it. In Jesus name

DAY 10

I am thankful for:

1.
2.
3.
4.
5.

"Give away your life; you'll find it given back, but not merely given back—given back with bonus and blessing. Giving not getting is the way." *(Luke 6:38 MSG)*

One of the best ways to live life to the fullest is to continually ask ourselves, "how can I give life to the person who I am with right now?" In every conversation, we can listen and encourage. Sometimes, we can even meet a need. We can live to give!

When we feel down, encouraging someone else makes us feel better. We think that we are helping others, and we are, yet this crazy thing happens—we get life given back to us "with bonus and blessing." Giving is always worth it.

What would change if we daily asked ourselves, "Who can I give life to?" This question will be added to each day.

God, help me to look around and see who needs encouragement or help. When I feel down, remind me to reach out to encourage those around me. In Jesus name

Who can I give life to today?

DAY 11

This makes my life fun:

1.
2.
3.
4.
5.

"...grasp the immensity of this glorious way of life he has for his followers, oh, the utter extravagance of his work in us who trust him—endless energy, boundless strength!" (Ephesians 1:16 MSG)

Grasp... Grasp means to hold on tight. What do you hold on to?

Choosing to grasp on to God's "way of life" for us means submitting to what God has for us. To submit to Him, we must trust His heart. His heart for us is good. He wants us to GRASP the life He has for us. At times, God's plans don't make sense to us in the moment or in our current situation. "God always has a bigger and better plan than we could dream up." (Lexie Fish)

Trusting His heart means trusting Him more than the plan we are hoping for. Are there circumstances in your life that make it difficult to let go of what I want and trust God? Trusting God is a choice, we do not have to let our feelings determine what we choose. We may not *feel* like trusting God, but we can choose to give Him control.

God, show me what You have for me. I want to, *"grasp the immensity of this glorious way of life,"* that you have for us. In Jesus name

Who can I give life to today?

DAY 12

What makes me laugh?

1.
2.
3.

"...let us do good to ALL people..." (Galatians 6:10 NIV)

Laughter is great and so powerful. We need to be around people who make us smile and laugh. At a memorial service yesterday, I heard a phrase that stuck with me, "everywhere he went, he made that place better." What a great thing to be said about someone. What if everywhere we went, we made that place better because we were there. Our words, our attitude, our thoughts, the way we make others feel can give life to others, which results in us enjoying life.

Who can I encourage or enjoy today?

God, help me to make life better for those around me by the way I encourage them. Help me to live full of Your love, so I can give it away. In Jesus name

Who can I give life to today?

DAY 13

What are 5 great things in my life?

1.
2.
3.
4.
5.

"Neither height nor depth, nor anything else in all creation will be able to separate us from the love of God that is in Christ Jesus our Lord." (Romans 8:39 NIV)

A repetitive negative thought doesn't help us. Instead it distracts us, ruins our day, and keeps us on a negative spiral.

If we find ourselves thinking the same negative thoughts we have to identify them and realize it's not helpful! Most negativity is wrapped up in the comparison trap. When we see someone who has what we don't, we are reminded of what we lack and start to focus on how we fall short. Comparing ourselves to others never helps our thinking. We never win when we are constantly playing the "comparison game."

What is one negative thought I am repetitively thinking? Am I comparing myself to others in this area?

In God's eyes we are all perfect, just how He made us. Thinking about God's love and acceptance of us is motivating. Changing our negative thoughts about ourselves and inviting Jesus in to this process will create joy and a more positive attitude.

God, I think about _____. I give this negative thought or feeling up to You. Motivate me to let this thought go and accept Your great love. In Jesus name

Who can I give life to today?

What progress can I celebrate today? (Where have I bettered myself? What have I consistently worked on? What habits am I changing?)

1.
2.
3.

"Celebrate God, all day, everyday..." (Philippians 4:4 MSG)

Everyday, we can start off the day celebrating God and all that He has given us. We can also celebrate progress. Reflecting back on progress and celebrating it is so powerful!

My kids work with an amazing tennis coach. She is always focused on progress instead of winning. Constantly improving is one of the main goals. She told my son something very motivating. If you improve 1% a month, in two years, you will have improved 25%. If you keep improving at this rate, you can reach your goals.

This is so LIFE-GIVING! In our current culture, we are conditioned to want everything immediately. We want quick results, which can cause a lot of stress. What if we focused on improving a little each day, each week, each month? We can celebrate progress, while we are reaching our goals and dreams.

God, help me to find my identity in YOU. As I work hard, help me to focus on progress. Remind me to celebrate You and life. In Jesus name

Who can I give life to today?

What is GOOD in my life?

1.
2.
3.
4.
5.

"It is for freedom that Christ has set us free. Stand firm.." (Galatians 5:1 NIV)

We all have something we wrestle with. I have never met a person that said "I don't struggle with anything." If someone did say this, I would bet they struggle with pride.

We all are tempted. What do we do with temptation?

When we are struggling, we have to choose to get better. This is at least 60% of winning the battle. When we choose to stand up to our struggle and decide to work on conquering it, we get better! Some struggles take longer to conquer than others. Over the last twenty years of counseling I have seen hundreds of teens.

I could not make any of them choose to get better from anxiety, depression, addiction, past pain...The students who got better were the ones who wanted to and chose it. It sounds simple. If we want to get better, we will, because we will find tools to help us, we will change our thoughts, we will pray about it, we will find ways to fight it, we will seek help. Christ set us free, we can live out our freedom if we choose to.

Jesus, I choose to start the process of healing from _____. Help me change my thoughts. Give me strength to change. Bring people to help guide me. In Jesus name

Who can I give life to today?

DAY 16

What am I thankful for?

1.
2.
3.
4.
5.

"Let God transform you into a new person by changing the way you think. Then you will learn to know God's will for you, which is good and pleasing and perfect." (Romans 12:2 NLT)

There are days we don't feel thankful. We wake up tired. Something hard is going on. We can't think of anything to be thankful for. We just don't feel it. On those days it is harder to choose great thoughts. It feels like a battle all day. Sometimes we just want to give up and let all that negativity win.

On days like this, a constant conversation with God is needed. We can invite Him into what is bothering us, our disappointment, our feelings, our yuck... Next, we can refocus every time our brain goes negative. We can think of the great. If we still feel stuck in sad feelings, we can start texting or messaging friends—encourage someone else. When we reach out to others we don't stay stuck in negative thoughts. We get to choose our day, just because our day starts off bad, it doesn't have to stay that way.

Jesus, I invite You into my day, my thoughts, my conversations, the messages I tell myself. Help me to choose to think about what is good in my life. In Your name

Who can I give life to today?

5 things that make me smile:

1.
2.
3.
4.
5.

"But the fruit of the Spirit is love, joy, peace, patience, kindness, goodness, faithfulness, gentleness, and self-control." (Galatians 5:22 NIV)

Small things mean a lot to people: an encouraging text, a smile, a thank you, a small gift. Those little choices—to give—make someone's day better. Doing small things for others takes the focus off of ourselves and the things that get us down.

What small thing can I do today to make someone's day better?

God, show me who needs encouragement. Help me to remember the seemingly small is not small to You. Show me Your heart for me. In Jesus name

Who can I give life to today?

DAY 18

I am thankful for:

1.
2.
3.
4.
5.

"...Embracing what God does for you is the best thing you can do for him. Don't become so well-adjusted to your culture that you fit into it without even thinking. Instead, fix your attention on God. You'll be changed from the inside out." (Romans 12:1-2 MSG)

What does "embracing" what God is doing look like?

At every stage in life we can live in an attitude of thankfulness, choose to bless others and invite Jesus in. This sounds really simple, but there are so many situations when it's not that easy to feel thankful. It is not always easy to bless others, especially if they are not kind to us. When we get anxious about life or the future, we can forget to invite Jesus in.

- Embracing what God is doing is about choosing an attitude of trust that God's heart for us is good.
- Embracing what God is doing *for us* involves forgiving others when they let us down and extending grace.
- Embracing what God is doing *in us* involves a choice instead of trying to figure it out alone, asking and inviting Jesus into every thought, decision, worry, relationship, dream and more.

May we embrace the life HE has for us today!

God, I invite You into all aspects of my life and I choose to trust YOUR heart for me. In Jesus name

Who can I give life to today?

What are 5 things you enjoy?

1.
2.
3.
4.
5.

"...Many people noticed the signs He was displaying and seeing they pointed straight to God, entrusted their lives to Him..." (John 3:23-25 MSG)

When I read the stories of when Jesus walked here on Earth I often wonder what His voice sounded like. What about Him drew a huge crowd? When He looked at people did they feel truly loved and treasured in such a way it made them want to follow Him for days?

We can take Bible stories and ask ourselves questions about Jesus. We learn more about His love for us when we stop and think about how He made the people around him feel.

One question we can ourselves when we read about him is, "What was His loving response to people who were not loving to Him?"

God in His compassion sent Jesus to show us a loving God who cares about our stuff.

Jesus, please show me more of who You are. In Jesus name

Who can I give life to today?

DAY 20

I love: (some of your favorite people or things)

1.
2.
3.
4.
5.

When we live in the truth that we are loved by the heart of God, His love fills our heart and spills out on others. These verses define love:

"Love cares more for others than for self.
Love doesn't want what it doesn't have.
Love doesn't strut,
Doesn't have a swelled head,
Doesn't force itself on others,
Isn't always 'me first,'
Doesn't fly off the handle,
Doesn't keep score of the sins of others,
Doesn't revel when others grovel,
Takes pleasure in the flowering of truth,

Puts up with anything,.
Trusts God always,
Always looks for the best,
Never looks back,
But keeps going to the end.
Love never dies." *(1 Corinthians 13 MSG)*

Looking at these verses we can ask ourselves these questions:

- How well am I loving those around me?
- Am I caring about and encouraging the people in my life?
- Do I spend more time gossiping and talking negatively about people behind their back, than I do I lifting people up?
- Would my friends consider me a safe person to talk to?
- What kind of friends do I want? How can I be that kind of friend to others?

God, please fill my heart with Your love so I can give Your love to others.

Who can I give life to today?

DAY 21

What makes my life good?

1.
2.
3.
4.
5.
6.
7.
8.
9.
10.

"Trust in the Lord with all your heart.." (Proverbs 3:5 NIV)

What in my life is hard to trust God completely with?

Why?

God's heart for us is good, so we can trust that His plans for us are good. When we face what we are not trusting Him with, it is easier to choose to let go. Trust, at times, is a choice, not a feeling. It might even involve a leap of faith.

God, I choose to trust You with _____,
because You are good and You love me. In Jesus name

Who can I give life to today?

What makes my life GREAT?

1.
2.
3.
4.
5.

"Are you tired? Worn out? Burned out on religion? Come to me. Get away with me and you'll recover your life. I'll show you how to take a real rest. Walk with me and work with me—watch how I do it. Learn the unforced rhythms of grace. I won't lay anything heavy or ill-fitting on you. Keep company with me and you'll learn to live freely and lightly." (Matthew 11:28-30 MSG)

When this verse states, "Keep company with me," it is talking about our relationship with Jesus. We can tell him about our day, or what bothered us or made us laugh. The more we talk to Him the more we understand His closeness. It's less about one daily, routine prayer, but a continual conversation with Him.

How does He talk back? Things He speaks to our spirit can echo repeatedly. So if we like a word, or we feel like He gives us a word like trust, faith, rest, change, or freedom, we can think about that word and what it means and how it applies in every area of our life. When we read The Bible, a verse or story can apply to our exact situation. This is Him keeping "company" with us and lighting a path for us to follow. We can personalize a verse, dissecting what it would mean in every area of our lives. His Spirit speaking to us never contradicts the Bible.

For instance, in the verse above, what does "live freely and lightly" mean? What would this look like in every area of your life?

Taking scripture and personalizing it to our lives helps us in our understanding of a relationship with Jesus.

God, I want to come to You and "keep company" with You. Show me what this looks like in my life. In Jesus name

Who can I give life to today?

DAY 23

What are five amazing things in your life?

1.
2.
3.
4.
5.

This is a secret to an amazing life. It is so simple, yet it changes everything!

1. Ask yourself, "What negative thoughts do I replay about myself?" I am guessing this thought affects everything you do, it did for me.
2. When that negative thought starts in your brain, say, "STOP!" The thought stops.
3. Think a great "go to" thought about you.

For example: I am a child of God, God has great things planned for me, I am a champion, I am a treasure, I am loved. Or find a song with great lyrics.

At age 19 I started doing this. My "go to" thought was, "define myself radically as one beloved by God, His love defines my worth" (paraphrased quote in Abba's Child by Brennan Manning). I must have told myself that phrase thousands of times to combat the negative thoughts I constantly battled.

Repeat steps 1–3 over and over again.

These steps will change your life FOREVER!

God, help me to take my thoughts back by thinking great things about life, You, and me. In Jesus name

Who can I give life to today?

DAY 24

What do I love about life?

1.
2.
3.
4.
5.

"Preach the Gospel at all times. When necessary, use words." (St. Francis of Assisi)

If we are growing in our relationship with God and finding ourselves wrapped in His love others will notice. Something about spending time with God transforms us from the inside out. This mystery of Christ working deep inside of us can change the world around us. If we are thinking great, thankful thoughts and inviting Jesus into every aspect of our lives, then our lives will reflect Jesus. We will be sharing the Gospel without even realizing it.

Does my life share Jesus in the way I talk to people, what I post or wear, and how I treat others?

God, show me more of Your great love. I invite Jesus into my conversations, my worries, my relationships, my thoughts, my dreams, my struggles, my hopes, my insecurities, my school and work.

Who can I give life to today?

DAY 25

God, thank You for:

1.
2.
3.
4.
5.

"...Keep a smile on your face." (Romans 12:8 MSG)

Choosing life to the fullest personally (for ourselves) is also about giving life to others. Smiling is one way to do this. A simple smile gives a kind message. We can continually look for ways to do and say good things to others. What does this do for us?

It takes the focus off of us and our stuff, our worries, our insecurities... When we look for ways to reach out to others, we don't have time to think about the negative.

What are ways that I can give life to others today?

God, help me to smile and reach out to others, especially when I don't feel like it. Remind me throughout the day to focus on the good gifts in my life. In Jesus name

Who can I give life to today?

DAY 26

What are three things that make my life GREAT?

1.
2.
3.

"It's in Christ that we find out who we are and what we are living for."
(Ephesians 1:11)

What do I do with failure? What happens when I encounter setbacks?

There are a few different ways we can respond to failure: we can quit, letting failure win, we can sit and resist trying again, we can let failure define us and decide we don't like ourselves, we can stop trying—or we can embrace failure and learn from it. We can look back at our progress, get up and get going, encouraged that we are one step closer to succeeding. Failure does not need to define us. Failing leads us one step closer to succeeding.

In sports, we see this often. During the course of a baseball game, a hitter can strike out, which looks like a failure. The next time he is up to bat he can renew his mind, take a deep breath and get a hit, maybe even hit a home run.

Do I let failure define me?

As the verse above stated, *"It's in Christ that we find out who we are and what we are living for."* By finding ourselves and our identity in Christ, we will not let failure or success define us.

God, help me to define myself as one beloved by God. Help me to know Your heart and that You have great things for me. In Jesus name

Who can I give life to today?

DAY 27

What am I thankful for?

1.
2.
3.
4.
5.

"Trust in the Lord with all your heart; do not depend on your own understanding. Seek His will in all you do, and He will show you which path to take." (Proverbs 3:5-6 NLT)

Trust is a choice, not a feeling. Feelings only have power to tell us what to do, if we let them. We can choose to trust God's heart for us in every area.

What is hard for you to trust God with? Why?

Then we can seek Him. Seeking Him involves inviting Him into situations, relationships, decisions, dreams and obstacles. Seeking Him leads to understanding and clear direction. Seeking God helps us trust His heart.

God, help me to TRUST You even when I don't feel like it. I choose to invite You into my thoughts, relationships, dreams, struggles, and decisions. In Jesus name

Who can I give life to today?

DAY 28

What can I celebrate today?

1.
2.
3.

"Celebrate God all day everyday." *(Philippians 4:4 MSG)*

God wants us to be people that celebrate Him and the life He has given us!

We can get so caught up in tasks and destinations that we forget to CELEBRATE the small steps, the progress, the little accomplishments. We can drive ourselves so hard that we lose focus on enjoying the moments *while* we are working hard. Celebrating progress can help keep joy thriving. Celebrating can be as small as getting an ice cream, going to a movie, taking a day to do something you enjoy, spending time with a friend and so much more!

So, let's celebrate! Our growth in our faith, our progress at school or work, our relational depth, our work at our hobby or sport, find something worth celebrating and take a moment to enjoy it.

God, I celebrate YOU, thank You for every gift You have given me. Help me to celebrate growth in my life. In Jesus name

Who can I give life to today?

DAY 29

What am I thankful for?

1.
2.
3.
4.
5.

"Above all, love each other deeply, because love covers a multitude of sins."
(1 Peter 4:8 NIV)

Is _____ (my choice) loving?

We can let one question lead us in every relationship, "Is this loving?"

We can further ask ourselves:

- Is this comment I want to say loving?
- Is what I want to do loving?
- Am I thinking of the other person, or myself?

In friendships we can get so caught up in being right that we stop thinking of the other person and start thinking about us. The questions above can help guide you to choose the person, not the argument. In a fight, if you "win" what cost did it come at? Winning by making someone you love lose, doesn't really feel like a success. In an argument we can focus on the person instead of the issue.

It is said that as Christ-followers we will be known by our LOVE. This love flows from the heart of God into our hearts. He has unconditional amazing love for us! His love is enough to fill our heart so we can give His love to others. If we need more love, we can ASK Him for it.

How can I love better today?

God, It is not easy to be loving all the time. Please give me more of YOU in my life. In Jesus name

Who can I give life to today?

DAY 30

What are 3 things that make me smile?

1.
2.
3.

"Cast all your anxiety on Him because He cares for you." (1 Peter 5:7 NIV)

Cast means "to throw." God wants us to throw Him all the things we are worried about. Anxiety is at a high in America, and especially among teens. One of the best ways to deal with anxiety is to make a daily list of all of the things that make us anxious and give them to God in prayer. We get to throw Him all our worries, but we don't need to take them back. Instead, we can ask for His peace. Trusting God's heart for us is key in giving Him the things we are anxious about. This practice of casting anxiety on Him is life-changing.

What am I anxious about?

God, I trust Your heart for me. I give YOU my anxiety. Please give me Your peace in exchange. In Jesus name

Who can I give life to today?

DAY 31

What am I glad about?

1.
2.
3.
4.
5.

"His very breath and blood flow through us, nourishing us so that we will grow up healthy in God, robust in love." (Ephesians 4:16 MSG)

When we give our life to Christ, He lives in us. His "very breath" is in us. Yet the world around us is so loud. There are distractions from every corner leading us away from the Truth, that in Him, we have everything we need.

If we look around us for real life, we will always be looking. Real life is found in a relationship with Jesus. He quenches something in our soul that nothing else can fill. We were created for a relationship with God, every other filler leaves us hungry for more. When I feel discontent or find myself spending a lot of time worrying, God gently reminds me that He is here and He is enough. He will take care of all of our worries and His love for each of us is bigger than the ocean. God is whispering His great love to all of us! We are given the choice, to listen to our feelings, or to listen to His truth. Real life is found living inviting Him into everything.

Jesus, life, stuff and temptation surround me, but You are the only things that can fulfill my life. Remind me of this often and help me to live in friendship with You. In Your name

Who can I give life to today?

What do I ENJOY?

1.
2.
3.
4.
5.

"Whatever is true...think on such things." (Philippians 4:8 NIV)

When I was a teenager my dad would quote Socrates to me, "The unexamined life is not worth living." What was he saying? He was reminding me to ask myself hard questions.

In his book "40 Days to a Joy Filled Life," Tommy Newberry talks about the life skill of reflection. His suggestion is for us to reflect by asking ourselves simple questions: "What has been working? What has not been working? What do I need to improve?"

In the last six weeks, what has been working? (relationally, spiritually, academically, in a sport or hobby)

What is not working? (In these same areas)

How can I improve?

Who can help me?

Do I need a change in my mindset?

If I feel overwhelmed, is the task really that difficult, or am I just telling myself negative messages?

Sometimes asking ourselves hard questions leads to discouragement, but instead of being discouraged, we can use it as a growing opportunity to make a shift in our actions and thoughts, and we can invite Jesus in to help us. If we never face what is not working, it is hard to make positive changes—facing the truth is LIFE GIVING!

God, help me to be honest with myself and give me the strength to make changes where I need to. In Jesus name

Who can I give life to today?

These are the GREAT things in my life:

1.
2.
3.
4.
5.

"And when you stand praying, if you hold anything against anyone, forgive them, so that your Father in heaven may forgive you your sins." *(Mark 11:25 NIV)*

Every few months I take a "forgiveness inventory" to keep my heart healthy. This means asking myself:

- Is there anyone who hurt my heart? Have I forgiven them?
- Has anyone let me down? Have I forgiven them?
- Am I thinking negative about anyone? Have I chosen to forgive and change my thoughts?

People let us down all of the time. Most of the time, it is not even about us, but about their own struggle, yet it still hurts. I encourage you to take your own forgiveness inventory. Choosing to forgive, whether you want to or not, feels so good. The result is freedom to be who God created us to be without walking around in bitterness.

God, I choose to forgive _____. I let go of the hurt that they caused me. Please help me to see this person through Your eyes of love. Clean my heart of all bitterness, pain, and resentment. Replace those things with Your JOY. In Jesus name

Who can I give life to today?

DAY 34

What makes me happy?

1.
2.
3.
4.
5.

"Who makes everything complete, Who fills everything everywhere with Himself." (Ephesians 1:23 AMPC)

This verse is talking about Jesus, I had to read it twice. He "fills." So many of us look for false fillers—achievement, approval, food, social media, success, relationships, addiction...

If there is an emptiness inside of us, it's because the love of Jesus is yet to fill that canyon in our souls. If you know about God or grew up in church you might have given your life to Jesus by saying, "I believe in You (Your death on the cross and resurrection), please forgive me for my sins, and I place my trust and life in your hands." At that moment, we became Christians. However, the Christian life is a journey. Some of us have asked God into our hearts, but have forgotten about that prayer of surrender. Or maybe our negative thoughts seem louder than God.

Do I ever feel empty?

What do I use to fill that void?

Jesus continually fills us with His love, His hope, and His joy. It is our choice to dive into His love, choose our thoughts, and invite Him in to fill everything in our life.

God, I want to embrace Your love, choose Your thoughts, and invite You in to "fill everything" in my life. In Jesus name

Who can I give life to today?

DAY 35

What are five GREAT things in my life?

1.
2.
3.
4.
5.

"Look carefully, then, how you walk. Live purposefully." *(Ephesians 5:1 AMPC)*

We can start the day right! The challenge is thinking about the great over and over and over again, even when we don't feel like it. Feelings don't have to be determiners of our thoughts. But sometimes we choose to let them.

For instance, we can wake up feeling grouchy, insecure or anxious, but we don't have to let our feelings choose the way we're going to think and act for the rest of the day. Just because we feel a certain way doesn't mean we have to live it out. Our thoughts get to tell our feelings what to do. So if we wake up feeling discouraged we can choose to think about all the great things in our life and ask God to take away the discouragement and give us joy.

Feelings don't get to control our thoughts. This mindset requires repetition—choosing a lifestyle of thinking about the things we are thankful for and inviting Jesus into our struggles. People who choose this healthy thinking lifestyle wake up one day and realize they are more positive and healthy and have more joy in their life!

God, I don't always feel it, but I want to choose thoughts that will bring me a great life, I invite Jesus into my feelings, my thoughts, my struggles. In His name

Who can I give life to today?

DAY 36

What is good in my life?

1.
2.
3.
4.
5.

"Come to Me, all you who are weary and burdened, and I will give you rest." (Matthew 11:28 NIV)

We can "come" to God when life is easy or difficult. Sometimes we don't though. We keep our stuff, we worry, we let the doubts and the "what ifs" swirl. When I do this, I don't even realize I am letting life get stressful.

If we are having a hard time concentrating or we feel overwhelmed, we can stop for a moment. Identify our stressors. Whisper a prayer giving God all of the things swirling in our brain. In exchange, He gives us the gift of inner peace, which makes our brain feel a sense of rest.

What am I worried about? What thoughts swirl in my head?

God, here are all of the things I can't stop thinking and worrying about. I invite You in to each of these situations. Please give me Your peace in exchange. In Jesus name

Who can I give life to today?

What am I excited about?

1.
2.
3.
4.
5.

(With God's help) "Take your everyday, ordinary life—your sleeping, eating, going-to-work, and walking-around life—and place it before God as an offering. Embracing what God does for you is the best thing you can do for him. Don't become so well-adjusted to your culture that you fit into it without even thinking. Instead, fix your attention on God. You'll be changed from the inside out. Readily recognize what he wants from you, and quickly respond to it." (Romans 12:1-2 MSG)

We are called to something greater everyday. We are called past the ordinary to extraordinary. How do we live extraordinary lives? Inviting Jesus into every area of our lives, thinking great over and over again, and reaching out to others are a few ways to make our lives extraordinary. We were each placed in our unique situation, with our unique gifts, to share in God's bigger story.

There is a bigger purpose for our lives, nothing is ordinary.

God, What do You have for me today? I invite You into every area of my life. May my thoughts stay on great things. Who can I reach out to today? In Jesus name

Who can I give life to today?

Who are five people that make me smile?

1.
2.
3.
4.
5.

"People don't need information: they want examples. God wants to use people like us to show the world what we know about Jesus by having them see the way we love the people around us." (Everybody Always, Bob Goff)

I started thinking about people who give life to me and make me smile—they have a lot of similarities! What do people who make you smile have in common?

The people who make me smile greet me with a smile or a word of encouragement, laugh a lot instead of getting stressed, and are real and not fake. These people also wait for an answer when they ask a question, are secure enough in themselves to be encouraging and excited when others around them succeed, they enjoy life, regardless of their circumstances and live like Jesus.

I want to be a person that makes others smile, don't you?

One cure to boredom is to reach out and think of ONE way to make someone else's day better. The result is our day also gets better! Making others smile actually makes us smile! Living life to the FULLEST is all about giving life to others and asking God to help us know how to do this.

Who can I give life to today? Who can I make smile?

God, show me who needs a smile, an encouraging word, or even a joke. When I get consumed with my own stuff, remind me to smile and give life to others. In Jesus name

Who can I give life to today?

DAY 39

What is great in my life?

1.
2.
3.
4.
5.

Who needs me to send a message of encouragement?

"Meanwhile, the moment we get tired in the waiting, God's Spirit is right alongside helping us along. If we don't know how or what to pray, it doesn't matter. He does our praying in and for us, making prayer out of our wordless sighs, our aching groans. He knows us far better than we know ourselves...and keeps us present before God. That's why we can be so sure that every detail in our lives of love for God is worked into something good." (Romans 8:26-28 MSG)

"He knows us far better than we know ourselves." We know what we want and what we think we need, but God knows our heart because He made it. Two things about this passage amaze me— one, God knows what we need so we can trust Him with today

and tomorrow, and two, He works "every detail of our lives into something good".

EVERY detail—that is amazing! Our struggles and our successes worked into something good. Our heartache and joys worked into something good.

Life does not always feel good. Yet, when we live communicating with God, we realize He is for us, He loves us, He knows us better than we know ourselves. When we get stressed, whispering a prayer and remembering God will work our life for good is key in living life to the fullest!

Do I give God my stress throughout the day or do I carry it?

Do I believe He will work EVERY detail out for my good?

God, I choose to trust Your heart for me. I give You _____. Please work this for my good. In Jesus name

Who can I give life to today?

What memory makes me smile? (Focusing on great memories reminds us that life is GREAT!)

"Let us not become weary in doing good..." (Galatians 6:9 NIV)

Sometimes we feel great. When we love life, it's easy to feel joyful, we want to give to and help others. Other times we feel tired, sad or blah, and the people around us can get on our nerves. Our *feelings* can change with circumstances, but we don't *have* to listen to them. Our feelings don't tell us what to do, our *thoughts* do! We get to choose to silence our feelings by thinking great about life. When we think great about our life, feelings start to change. Our thoughts control our feelings.

A way to apply this to our lives is if we are feeling sad, we can think of great things in our life, do something kind for someone else, and think of things we are thankful for. This leads to a change in our feelings of hope and gratitude. Some days when we don't feel it, we just need to keep going. Keep thinking GREAT and inviting Jesus in!

God, remind me of Your truths and help my feelings to follow. I invite YOU into my thoughts. In Jesus name

Who can I give life to today?

DAY 41

What do I like about myself?

1.
2.
3.
4.
5.

Thinking about our strengths inspires, in contrast, focusing on our weaknesses demotivates. To like ourselves through the ups and downs we must know that we are made in God's image.

"In the image of God, he created him; male and female He created them. God blessed them..." (Genesis 1:27-28 NIV)

God made us in His image. We can like ourselves because the Creator of the Universe likes us. Something mysterious happens inside of us when we choose to accept God's love and communicate with Him. Talking to God about life changes our day.

One practical way to connect with God is to spend time in prayer, read his word and journal (PB&J).

1. Pray: Talk to God about the things that are bothering you, or tell him things you are thankful for.
2. Bible: Read a Bible verse and think about how it applies to your life.
3. Journal: Write down any insights from this time.

Have you ever thought about this, since we are made in the image of God when He looks at us He smiles like a proud parent, because we resemble Him.

God, I need to remember my worth comes from the fact that You made me and You love me. Remind me of this often. In Jesus name

Who can I give life to today?

What things make my life GREAT?

1.
2.
3.
4.
5.

"Come to me, all you who are weary and burdened and I will give you rest." (Matthew 11:28 NIV)

After you do the three steps from yesterday, quiet yourself for a minute. Stop the swirl—all of the thoughts of worry and things you have to do. Think about a verse you read. Today the verse above is, "come to Me." In the quiet moments, we can choose to hear His whisper and let the words of the Bible echo in our minds. This is one way God speaks to us. What do we need to give to God today?

God, I come to You today bringing a lot of thoughts and worries, please take them. In Jesus name

Who can I give life to today?

DAY 43

What can I thank God for?

1.
2.
3.
4.
5.

"And now, dear brothers and sisters, one final thing. Fix your thoughts on what is true, and honorable, and right, and pure, and lovely, and admirable. Think about things that are excellent and worthy of praise." (Philippians 4:8 NLT)

Living life to the fullest is about choosing to make our mind stay on the things that are true. What is true? God loves us, He made us, He has a plan for us, His heart for us is good, He calls us a masterpiece, He treasures us. Nothing can separate us from His love.

Do my thoughts stay on truths or feelings?

God, Help me to remember Who YOU are and who You say I am. Help me to remember I can choose good and true thoughts that make my life GREAT! In Jesus name

Who can I give life to today?

DAY 44

What do I love about life?

1.
2.
3.
4.
5.

"So all of us who have had that veil removed can see and reflect the glory of the Lord. And the Lord—who is the Spirit—makes us more and more like him as we are changed into his glorious image." (2 Corinthians 3:8 NLT)

If you have been to the lake or ocean recently, you probably have seen the sun reflected on the water. We reflect "the glory of God." The way we do life and treat others can be a reflection of God. When others look at our life, they can see Jesus by the way we treat them. We can share His love by the things we post, the words we speak, and the way we make others feel. When we leave a conversation, we can have a goal to make the person we are spending time with feel better about life after spending time with us. Reading about Jesus when He walked on Earth, we can see that He gave love and compassion everywhere He went. We can reflect Him by the way we treat others and do life.

Do I reflect God in the way I do life?

God, I want to reflect You. I invite You into my thoughts. In Jesus name

Who can I give life to today?

What do I like about myself? (no negatives!)

1.
2.
3.
4.
5.

"Look! I stand at the door and knock. If you hear my voice and open the door, I will come in, and we will share a meal together as friends." (Revelation 3:20 NLT)

We go through so many doors each day. We make the choice to open them. When we see a friend at our door knocking, we excitedly unlock the door, immediately opening it to invite them in. God wants a friendship with us, He wants us to invite him in, just like we do our friends.

This verse gives insight to our walk with Jesus. He is always pursuing a friendship with us. However, He is not barging His way through. He waits. We don't have to beg Him to come into our life or our situation, He is already there waiting to be invited! Jesus wants to be invited into our life, our thoughts, our situations, our moments, our dreams, our relationships, our worries, our insecurities, our routines, our future...His heart for us is good! We get to choose our thoughts and we get to choose to open the door to Him. Even if we do not totally understand Him, we can invite Him in and begin a friendship with Him.

Jesus, I open the door to You. I invite You into every area of my life. Show me Your heart of friendship for me. In Your name

Who can I give life to today?

DAY 46

What am I thankful for today?

1.
2.
3.
4.
5.

A few weeks ago, I wrote about picking a motivating word to own for this season or the semester. If you picked a word, how is it going? Is your word motivating you? Do you need to find a new word? Sometimes we need to readjust. If you feel like the word you picked isn't encouraging you, pick a new one!

God is always whispering encouragement to us. If we read His words we can hear them echo throughout the day. His Spirit guides us. *"The Spirit of Truth, he will guide you into all truth." (John 16:12 NIV)*

Last summer, my word was "enjoy." I continually asked myself, "how do I enjoy this moment, living it to the fullest?" Or I whispered a prayer, "God, show me how to live in joy each moment." Throughout the day, I think about the word I chose for this season, asking God what it means in different situations. Throughout the day we can ask God, "Show me what to do or say in this situation. Show me how to live (our word) in each situation." In Jesus name

Who can I give life to today?

DAY 47

What am I thankful for?

1.
2.
3.
4.
5.

"You'll be your best by filling your minds and meditating on things TRUE..." (Philippians 4:8 MSG)

The continual battle of thinking great is real! We wake up in the morning and get to invite God into our day and be thankful and filled with gratitude. Then we get stuck in traffic, we are running late for school or work, or somebody says or posts something mean...derailing our day. Maybe we started off the day thinking great but immediately, because of life stuff, we go to a negative place. But if, and when, we go to a negative place in our mind, we don't have to stay there. No one can ruin our day. No circumstance can destroy our day. Even on the worst of days we can think of great things in our life and choose kindness to others. In the middle of a challenging day or hour, remembering the truth that God loves us and He is for us—can change everything!

God, in the middle of these situations, stop me from spiraling into negativity. Help me to think about Your truth continually. In Jesus name

Who can I give life to today?

DAY 48

What do I enjoy?

"A joyful heart is good medicine..." (Proverbs 17:22 ESV)

Much of my life, my dad told me, "life is a marathon, not a sprint, ENJOY the journey." What keeps us from enjoying the journey? Worry can keep us from enjoying the journey. We worry about what others are thinking. We worry about whether we are good enough for the goal that we are striving to reach. We worry thinking, "do I have what it takes?" We worry about tomorrow.

Worry steals moments of JOY. Enjoying the journey consists of inviting God into our journey, fully living each moment, and being our very best in that moment. We live in a society where we are all striving to reach the top, but are we having any fun on the journey? So many amazing talented people quit their dream, because stress consumes them. Exchanging JOY for worry is essential. If we choose to enjoy the journey instead of focusing on the destination, one day we will look around and realize that we are living a FULL life.

Do I enjoy each day or am I pushing myself so hard that my life is not fun?

God, help me to invite You into my thoughts, my words, my moments, my dreams, my journey. I choose Your joy instead of my worry. In Jesus name

Who can I give LIFE to today?

Who can I give life to today?

DAY 49

What are 10 great things in my life

1.
2.
3.
4.
5.
6.
7.
8.
9.
10.

"On your feet now—applaud God!
Bring a gift of laughter..." (Psalms 100:1-2 MSG)

We get to choose great thoughts! We can think about the things we are excited about, great memories we have, fun celebrations, great friendships, what we hope for, and we can remember that God has good things for us!

Or...we can think not so great thoughts. We can think about what worries us, our financial struggles, we can replay our failures, the person who hurt our feelings, the feeling of rejection.

Each morning our very first thoughts can be light or dark. No one can choose for us. Let's have an amazing day!

God, I invite You into my thoughts. May I live life in continual thankfulness to YOU! In Jesus name

Who can I give life to today?

What is GREAT in my life?

1.
2.
3.
4.
5.

If I can't think of great things in my life, maybe it is because I want to "get away" or escape. If so, what do I want to get away from?

Maybe the routine, responsibilities, the boring, and mundane... but that stuff is all there when I get back.
So maybe it's not getting away from it ALL...
What if it's just changing my attitude about all of my life stuff?
What if I chose to like who I am and the life I have?
What if I embrace my day with excitement, my routines with excellence, my boring with a smile, and my responsibilities with an attitude of laughter?
What if we approached every day every moment and gave it our best?
What would change if we are all in no matter what we're doing?

What if we left every conversation, every task, every practice, every day...grinning because we gave it our all?

If we give our best attitude, our greatest effort, while enjoying every moment, thinking great about others, about God, about ourselves, we can live without regret. We can be "all in."

"He gives strength to the weary
and increases the power of the weak.
Even youths grow tired and weary,
and young men stumble and fall;
but those who hope in the Lord
will renew their strength.
They will soar on wings like eagles;
they will run and not grow weary,
they will walk and not be faint."
(Isaiah 40:29-31)

God, when I want a "day off" from life, remind me of all the great things in my life. Instead of hiding or running away, help me to jump in. Give me your "strength." Help me to always look for the good, and may finding the "good" in life give me energy and joy. In Jesus name

Who can I give life to today?

DAY 51

What are 10 Great things in my life?

1.
2.
3.
4.
5.
6.
7.
8.
9.
10.

"Examine and see how good the Lord is. Happy is the person who trusts the Lord." (Psalms 34:8 ICB)

When we list the great things in our life, we are choosing to focus on the good. When we thank God for all of the good, we develop a heart of gratitude. Gratitude becomes our attitude and we find ourselves thankful instead of expectant. To have a heart of gratitude means constantly thinking about the things that we are thankful for. We can do this every time our mind goes to a negative place. When we think about something that we dislike or that annoys us, immediately we can stop that thought and think of a great thing in our life. We can choose gratitude by thanking God for the good things and letting the negative go. When gratitude is our attitude others notice and enjoy us. Gratitude not only helps our own thinking, but it encourages those we do life with.

God, I trust YOU. Thank You for _____ (the good and great things) in my life. In Jesus name

Who can I give life to today?

DAY 52

Who can I thank?

1.
2.
3.
4.
5.

"Instead, fix your attention on God. You'll be changed from the inside out. Readily recognize what he wants from you, and quickly respond to it. Unlike the culture around you, always dragging you down to its level of immaturity, God brings the best out of you, develops well-formed maturity in you." (Romans 12:2 MSG)

Everyone longs for REAL. Being real with people means getting past the masks and not pretending what is really going on in our heart.

When I was sixteen, in the middle of a mess of perfectionism and people pleasing, with my self- esteem plummeting, hating what I faced in the mirror, I started going to counseling. My counselor described me as a statue trying to present a perfect image, wearing my sport's uniform, books in one hand, the other hand pointed to God, a smile plastered on my face. He said, "You are not real, everyone longs for real." At this point, I started crying. I had been trying so hard to keep up an image and have it all together. He further explained that when the statue started cracking, healing would come and this would actually be a strength instead of a weakness. Realness…

We all have real life stuff. Maybe we don't like ourselves, maybe we have a hidden secret, maybe we were wounded, maybe our home life is hard, maybe we have a broken dream, maybe we struggle with anxiety, depression, or destructive thoughts. Realizing I did not want to be a statue of a person gave me permission to be real with God and others. Realness was so freeing and what I realized along the way is that people long for realness. Perfectionism is annoying. It is hard to be a perfect but fake statue.

Finding someone to be REAL with is essential in living life to the fullest. We can't pretend our life stuff isn't there. We can face it and come up with a plan that will lead to enjoying life. Living thinking GREAT does not mean ignoring reality, it means facing the real, inviting God to heal the broken places, and choosing to think thoughts of HOPE and thankfulness.

What is your real life stuff? I encourage you to journal about it and find a wise friend or mentor (or parent) to share it with.

God, here is my real, my messy, my stuff_____.
I am tired of pretending. Heal my hurt and transform it into something beautiful. In Jesus name

Who can I give life to today?

DAY 53

What is good in my life?

1.

2.

3.

4.

5.

"Now God has us where he wants us, with all the time in this world and the next to shower grace and kindness upon us in Christ Jesus. Saving is all his idea, and all his work. All we do is trust him enough to let him do it. It's God's gift from start to finish! We don't play the major role. If we did, we'd probably go around bragging that we'd done the whole thing! No, we neither make nor save ourselves. God does both the making and saving. He creates each of us by Christ Jesus to join him in the work he does, the good work he has gotten ready for us to do, work we had better be doing." (Ephesians 2:8-10 MSG)

God will always help us. He wants us to "join" Him in what He is doing. If there is something we are struggling with it usually has a root or a reason. In high school, the eating disorder I struggled with was fueled by insecurity and the desire for perfection. Using the eating disorder to cope with the inner struggle became a ten-year habit starting before middle school. Once the root of my struggle was dealt with, it took a while to learn how to break unhealthy habits. Letting God walk beside me and heal me on the inside created complete freedom.

If you struggle with something, I encourage you to face it and find the source. When you feel tempted by your struggle, process the reason by journaling or writing out your thoughts.

What are you thinking?

What are you afraid of?

Did someone or something reject you?

What painful memory or message swirls in your brain?

What is the source or root of your struggle? (loneliness, sadness, anger, hurt, pressure)

If you identify the reason for the struggle, it is much easier to start changing the habits. Many years ago, God completely healed my eating disorder. However, it took longer and more work than I thought it would. Still, it was worth it. All the hard work of discovering the reason and then breaking bad habits needed to happen for me to live life to the fullest. The GRACE and KINDNESS of God is a gift, we must repeatedly accept His gift. To overcome our struggle, we must daily invite Him into our struggle.

Jesus, I need You to help me face what I am wrestling with and then I need You to defeat it. Give me strength to daily choose You and Your grace. In Your name

Who can I give life to today?

DAY 54

What is GREAT in my life?

1.
2.
3.
4.
5.

"So, chosen by God for this new life of love, dress in the wardrobe God picked out for you: compassion, kindness, humility, quiet strength, discipline. " (Colossians 3:12 MSG)

We are told to wear compassion as we interact with others. What is compassion? Vocabulary.com defines compassion as, "'a word for a very positive emotion that has to do with being thoughtful and decent. Giving to a charity takes compassion. Volunteering to work with sick people or animals takes compassion. When you have compassion, you're putting yourself in someone else's shoes and really feeling for them. Anytime a disaster like a hurricane or earthquake hits, others will feel compassion for the victims. When you feel compassion for someone, you really want to help out."

If we are only focused on our own needs or struggles, it is difficult to give compassion. When we give our stuff to God, we are freed up to reach out to others and see life through their eyes. Looking past ourselves to help others creates a deep feeling of joy inside of us. Choosing compassion helps us enjoy life.

Who can I show compassion to today by encouraging, listening to, or sending a text or message?

God, help me to look around and see who needs Your heart of compassion and help me to extend Your compassion to others. In Jesus name

Who can I give life to today?

DAY 55

5 things I love to see:

1.
2.
3.
4.
5.

"Open your mouth and taste, open your eyes and see—how good God is. Blessed are you who run to him." (Psalms 34:8 MSG)

How do we experience God here on earth? By relating to our own senses, this verse gives us a suggestion using the word "open." When we "open" our eyes to see something, we are looking more deeply, when we "open" our mouth we can savor a food we enjoy. When we continually open up our life to God, we grow in our relationship with Him. We can look at God and open up our eyes to Him by reading about Him in the Bible (specifically the books of Matthew, Mark, Luke, and John). While reading, we can ask ourselves what was God like when He walked here on Earth? Jesus put on skin to live among us, so by reading about him we can see what God is really like, and who He really is. We can open up our heart and mind to God by inviting Him to do life with us throughout each day.

Does anything hold me back from inviting God in? If so, what?

God, I invite You into my life (heart, mind, day, conversations, struggles, dreams) I open my eyes to You, show me more of who You are. In Jesus name

Who can I give life to today?

DAY 56

What are 5 things I love?

1.
2.
3.
4.
5.

"A new command I give you: Love one another. As I have loved you, so you must love one another. By this everyone will know that you are my disciples, if you love one another." (John 13:34-35 NIV)

Choosing to show love regardless of the circumstances makes Christianity appealing to others. We can all think of a person that is hard to show love to. Maybe this person is rude. Maybe this person is an outcast. Maybe this person makes it difficult to be kind to them. However, when we choose to love those who are not likable, others notice and wonder what is different about us to be able to extend grace and kindness to those who are not easy to love.

"Find a way to love difficult people more, and you'll be living the life Jesus talked about. Go find someone you've been avoiding and give away extravagant love to them." (Everybody Always, Bob Goff)

Who can I give extravagant love to today?

God, help me to choose to love like You do whether I feel like it or not. In Jesus name

Who can I give life to today?

DAY 57

I am thankful for:

1.
2.
3.
4.
5.

"Pray continually." (1 Thessalonians 5:17)

Prayer is a gift. We get to pray about the things that seem too big for us. We also get to pray about the small concerns. Instead of holding on to it, we can give God our stuff.

"Bold prayers honor God, and God honors bold prayers. God isn't offended by your biggest dreams or boldest prayers. He is offended by anything less." (Your Powerful Prayers, Susie Larson)

God cares about what we care about. This quote is not talking about praying to win the lottery, it is talking about asking God for things that are dear to our heart, to fix situations that seem impossible, and to help us accomplish things for His Kingdom.

When we pray about something we are choosing to let go of our control and worry and we are giving the situation to Him. Praying changes us. When we pray, we decide to let go and trust God. We can pray to God throughout the day about any situation.

God, I give You _____. You know and You care. I invite You in. In Jesus name

Who can I give life to today?

DAY 58

What is GREAT in my life?

1.
2.
3.
4.
5.

"We demolish arguments and every pretension that sets itself up against the knowledge of God, and we take captive every thought to make it obedient to Christ." (2 Corinthians 10:5 NIV)

"We demolish arguments!" Sometimes we have to argue with ourselves. Because of negative thinking habits or the enemy, we wrestle with defeating thoughts. Maybe we don't feel like we are enough, we wonder if we will ever get there, and we are so aware of our failures. The negatives echo in our mind. We have a *choice* to demolish all of this negativity trying to argue with who we really are, "a masterpiece, a treasure, a conqueror, a chosen generation, sons and daughters of God." We get to choose which thought to listen to. We don't have to let the negative beat us down. We can stop the self-defeating thoughts and focus on what God, the creator of the universe, says about us.

What is one thing God says about you that can be your "go to" thought when the negativity starts creeping in?

God, Help me to listen to what You call me, may Your voice drown out all the negativity, so I can live life to the FULLEST. In Jesus name

DAY 59

What am I thankful for:

1.
2.
3.
4.
5.

"So if the Son sets you free, you are truly free." (John 8:36 NLT)

FREE—we all want to be free from something. Free from guilt, worry, shame, anger, people-pleasing, struggles, fears, a specific memory...so how do we get free? Submitting to God is one of the hardest things to do. Submitting that thing or thought over and over again leads to freedom. The key to whatever binds us is submitting it and letting go, giving it to Him. Giving Him the struggle is not a one time thing. To live in freedom we might have to say this prayer over and over again.

What do I hold on to?

How can I give this to God?

Jesus, I give You _____. I can't fix this. I need You to set me free. In Jesus name

Who can I give life to today?

DAY 60

What am I hopeful for?

1.
2.
3.
4.
5.

"We have this hope as an anchor for the soul, firm and secure..." *(Hebrews 6:19 NIV)*

What does it mean to have hope?

When our hope is in Jesus, we realize that we have everything we need, right when we need it. Hope is a choice of believing that God is good and life will be okay. Hope tells us that even in our most difficult moments that everything will work out. Our foundation in Jesus gives us hope, anchors us, and stabilizes us. Hope doesn't make the pain go away, but it gives us peace through the pain.

What are some practical ways that I can grow in my hope in Jesus?

God, help me to choose to hope in You regardless of my circumstances. In Jesus name

Who can I give life to today?

DAY 61

What am I excited about?

1.
2.
3.
4.
5.

"Be still and know that I am God." (Psalms 46:10 NIV)

In our fast paced society, being still is so difficult. I am not good at being still, yet in the quiet God speaks to my heart. Through the years, I have gotten better at doing this. One of my favorite ways to hear God speak to my Spirit is quieting myself and reflecting on a verse like, *"For I know the plans I have for you, declares the Lord..." (Jeremiah 29:11)*

God whispers this one often when I am thinking, "what's next? How is this going to work? What does the future look like?" In the quiet, thinking about this verse, God told me. "I already know the plan for you (your family)." If God knows the plan and His heart is good, then I can rest in His plan. Owning this verse has brought me great peace.

Here is one way to be still:

1. Read a Bible verse or story that you like
2. Set your watch or phone for 2 minutes
3. Close your eyes and think about the verse or story you picked and how it applies to your life
4. Ask God to show you something about this verse/story
5. Write it down

When I started this practice, a wise mentor told me that God never contradicts Himself or His Word. If something comes to your mind but doesn't fall in line with Jesus's teachings, then it is not from God.

God, I invite You into my day, my thoughts, my time with You. Keep negativity and distraction away. In Jesus name

Who can I give life to today?

What do I enjoy?

1.
2.
3.
4.
5.

"Immense in mercy and with an incredible love, he embraced us."
(Ephesians 2:4 MSG)

I think God enjoys us! Here it says, "WITH INCREDIBLE LOVE."

Most of us push and drive ourselves too hard to achieve. Finding our identity in His love is the only safe basis for identity, because it never changes. Achievements change, we can win one day and lose the next. Yet God's love never changes and is a secure foundation for who we really are.

When life is crazy, to recenter myself I think about these truths until they sink down, calming all the other swirling thoughts. "God loves me and His heart for me is GOOD."

Do I live reminding myself that God has amazing incredible LOVE for me?

God, I want to base my identity on Your love. Remind me of Your love for me throughout each day. In Jesus name

Who can I give life to today?

DAY 63

What five things am I thankful for?

1.
2.
3.
4.
5.

What one person could I encourage today? _____

"...you know how to give good things to your children. How much more will your Father in heaven give good things to those who ask Him?" (Matthew 7:11 NLV)

I bought my teenage son, Owin, something he really wanted on eBay and I was so excited to give it to him, but UPS was running later than expected. When it did finally come in, his excitement made my whole day, which led me to think about how the Father loves to give good gifts to His children. But sometimes I'm not sure what the holdup is and why things are taking so long. His timing doesn't always make sense.

When He does give us the gift He has planned, I think He is excited. Have you ever watched someone open a surprise gift you knew they wanted? Their reaction is amazing! I can imagine God watching us when our eyes get big and we smile from ear to ear as we receive our gift. His heart is excited to give GOOD gifts to His children. God's heart for us is good and every good gift is from His hand. If He's not working within our time frame, there's a good reason. Which means we get the choice to trust that His heart for us is good.

Do I think God enjoys giving me gifts?

God, thank You for life. Thank You that Your heart for me is good. Help me to trust Your timing on the gifts that You give. In Jesus name

Who can I give life to today?

DAY 64

What is ONE thing I can be repeatedly thankful for today?

_____

Who can I give to, bless, or help today?

_____

"Jesus looked at them and said, 'With man this is impossible, but with God all things are possible.'" (Matthew 19:26 NIV)

Recently, I found my journal from my freshman year of college. In one journal entry, I was praying about the book I was writing that shared my journey and recovery from bulimia. Guess what? I never finished and published it, I chickened out! The voices in my head won. My negative thoughts told me no one would want to read and it wasn't good. Maybe I believed I had to be totally recovered and perfect to share my pain and journey to health. That year I wrote one hundred pages, but I never put it out there. It is in a box somewhere in the attic. Many years went by until I took the risk and published. I was afraid of my dream that God put in my heart. Are you ever afraid of your God-sized dream?

Through the years, my thoughts about God and myself changed. I was encouraged in a message by Jeff Henderson, our pastor at Gwinnett Church, to write on a sticker what only God could do. This sticker was placed on the church wall along with hundreds of other people's dreams and thoughts just like mine. Walking past this wall every Sunday for months and months gave me enough courage to trust God with a dream He put in my heart. Since college, I had been writing, but I did not want to risk rejection if I shared it. Maybe I worried too much about what people would think, or I thought my writing was too vulnerable, or I believed I had to write something bestseller material before putting it out there. I'm not really sure what held me back. Looking back, I wish I would've started sharing my faith through the avenue of writing a little bit earlier, because writing is life-giving to me! I want to encourage you if God puts something in your heart to do for Him—take a RISK, He will meet all Your needs along the way!

What is your God sized dream that will glorify Him?

What is holding you back?

God, I give You this dream I believe YOU placed in my heart— give me the courage to take a risk and lead me exactly where You want me to go. In Jesus name

Who can I give life to today?

DAY 65

What makes me smile? (A few of mine are: listening to a great song, watching a close game, moments with friends and family)

1.
2.
3.
4.
5.

"God is love." (1 John 4:8 NIV)

The heart of God—what is it like? God's heart is love. Thinking back through some Bible stories I can see God's heart is full of grace, forgiveness, and restoration. When God came to earth in human skin, in the form of Jesus, He was tender, yet strong. Everyone wanted to be with Him. He must have been wise, funny, caring, healing, gentle, powerful...Crowds would follow Him for days. His presence and voice must have fulfilled what every soul longed for. One reason He came to earth is to give us a clear picture of Who God is.

His heart is full of *"love, joy, peace, patience, kindness, goodness, faithfulness, gentleness, and self-control." (Galatians 5:22)*

The enemy of our soul tries to convince us that God is distant, frustrated, disappointed, or aloof. The enemy brings guilt and shame. In contrast, God brings forgiveness and love. What we think about God affects every aspect of life.

Do we live in the realization that God's heart for us is complete love and forgiveness?

God, show me Your heart, silence the enemy's lies. In Jesus name.

Who can I give life to today?

DAY 66

I am thankful for:

1.
2.
3.
4.
5.

Who can I text a message of encouragement to?

"The Lord is not slow in keeping his promise, as some understand slowness. Instead he is patient with you, not wanting anyone to perish, but everyone to come to repentance." (2 Peter 3:9 NIV)

I have been thinking a lot about stop signs and red lights. They are necessary and keep us from getting into wrecks, yet they slow me down from getting to my destination. Sometimes I need to be slowed down. Life is moving so fast and there is so much to do...right? Honestly, at times God doesn't move as fast as I want Him to.

When His timing is not our timing, we have a choice to trust His heart and grow in the waiting instead of running through the stop lights, rushing His plans, or resenting the way He is doing things and distancing ourselves.

God sees the big picture and He sees all the moving pieces we don't see. Therefore, the wise choice is trusting His heart for us and His plan for us.

What do I have a hard time trusting God with? Why?

God, I trust You with me. I choose to trust Your timing. In Jesus name

Who can I give life to today?

DAY 67

Who am I thankful for?

1.
2.
3.

"Stay with what you heard from the beginning, the original message. Let it sink into your life. If what you heard from the beginning lives deeply in you, you will live deeply in both Son and Father. This is exactly what Christ promised: eternal life, real life!" (1 John 2:24-25 MSG)

Real life—isn't that what we all want? Many search a lifetime for real life. In His complexity, God makes it so simple. Here this verse says, *"stay with what you heard from the beginning."* In church preschool, the message of the Gospel is so simple, "Jesus loves me." Jesus loves us and wants a growing friendship with us. This truth makes us lovable, whether we feel lovable or not.

Letting this truth "sink into our life" is the beginning of experiencing real life. Jesus loves us today in our _____ (success, struggle, anxiety, depression, whatever we are living in).

Embracing His love as our identity and what makes us special changes everything. This is REAL LIFE!

Jesus, I want real life, may I embrace the fact that You love me unconditionally. May Your love sink in my heart and mind creating real life and identity in You. In Jesus name

DAY 68

I am thankful for:

1.
2.
3.
4.
5.

"Give thanks in all circumstances." (1 Thessalonians 5:18)

Choosing thankfulness in "all circumstances"—even when life is not going well—is hard to do. Most of us don't feel thankful when life throws us curve balls. However, we get to choose our thoughts, which tell our feelings what to do. One helpful thing is developing a heart of compassion for others. When we look outside of ourselves, we can see other's hurts, their pain, their life stuff. When we do this we realize we are not alone—maybe their circumstances seem worse than ours and we can choose compassion. Compassion for others helps combat feeling sorry for ourselves when life is hard. This can lead to thankfulness.

Who in my life is struggling and how I can reach out to them today?

God, help me to choose thankfulness regardless of my circumstances. Show me someone who needs Your heart of compassion. In Jesus name

Who can I give life to today?

DAY 69

God, thank You for:

1.
2.
3.
4.
5.

"Your fellowship with God enables you to gain a victory over the Evil One. Don't love the world's ways. Don't love the world's goods. Love of the world squeezes out love for the Father." (1 John 2:14-15 MSG)

If we feel stuck in a struggle or sin, this verse explains how to combat our struggles and be victorious—fellowship with God. We don't use this word "fellowship" much, it simply means spending time in God's presence. Our souls are all hungry for something—what they crave is the love and tenderness of God. All the stuff in this world is a counterfeit, it just doesn't fill that inner longing. When I worked for Young Life, speakers used the visual of a glove to explain this concept. Only a hand can fill a glove, the glove is empty and cannot be filled or used until filled with a hand. Inviting Jesus into our life fills our life like the hand fills the glove. If we have a relationship with Jesus, how do we tap into His love daily? By carving out time to spend with Him, praying and reading the bible. At first this might seem boring or routine, but something in us awakens when we spend time developing our friendship with God.

God, help me to find a few minutes in my day to give to You. In those moments reveal Your heart to me. In Jesus name

Who can I give life to today?

DAY 70

What is GREAT in my life?

1.
2.
3.
4.
5.

"And now, children, stay with Christ. Live deeply in Christ. Then we'll be ready for him when he appears, ready to receive him with open arms, with no cause for red-faced guilt or lame excuses when he arrives." (1 John 2:28 MSG)

"Live deeply in Christ." What does this mean? So many of us grew up in church hearing all of the Bible stories, yet what does that look like as a student, in college, or adult life?

In high school, I remember feeling like God was keeping track of what I did or didn't do. This was a terrible motivator—I always felt like I could not do enough. Maybe you have felt this way. How do we gauge "living for" Christ?

When I was nineteen, God whispered to me, "I love you, because I made you, I, Jesus, love you." No ifs, ands, or buts...I thought I had already embraced this, but I hadn't, my Christian life up until this time was not love motivated. Instead, it was performance-motivated. Something in my brain and heart switched that day, a light came on!

The LOVE of God is something to embrace, to let soak into the core of who we are and drive away the shaming, shoulding, guilting thoughts—those will never keep us motivated. Staying motivated is a reflection of what we are thinking and telling ourselves daily. Focusing on truths about His heart can help us live thinking healthy.

For example:

1. God loves us completely because He made us
2. Jesus wants a friendship with us because to Him we are all lovable

What motivates me to live for God? (Am I motivated by love? Or are guilt and "shoulds" motivating me?)

God, I want Your love to soak into my heart. Show me what it means to find my identity and motivation in Your love. In Jesus name

Who can I give life to today?

DAY 71

Who is good to me?

1.
2.
3.

How can I thank them? (a simple thank you, a card, a text)

"So here's what I want you to do, God helping you: Take your everyday, ordinary life—your sleeping, eating, going-to-work, and walking-around life—and place it before God as an offering. Embracing what God does for you is the best thing you can do for him." (Romans 12:1-2 MSG)

What is my "everyday, ordinary?"

Sometimes we think that we have to wait for the BIG to serve God. Maybe we want a stage or we think we have to wait until we are out of college, or married, or have kids. Don't wait! We can start serving God in the ordinary today! In our "everyday, ordinary," we can treat people in our life extraordinarily! We can make someone else's day by making them feel special.

Do I live my "ordinary" with excellence?

Sometimes doing our ordinary life with kindness and excellence leads us to extraordinary. Who we are in the simple is who we really are.

What seemingly routine and boring things can I do today with kindness, joy, excitement, and excellence? Who will this bless?

God, life can feel boring—help me make life exciting by living those ordinary moments EXTRAORDINARY for You and those who you have placed around me. In Jesus name.

Who can I give life to today?

DAY 72

What gives me joy?

1.
2.
3.
4.
5.

"What, then, shall we say in response to these things? If God is for us, who can be against us?" (Romans 8:31 NIV)

"It's never too late to do the right thing." As a student confronted with life stuff, my mom would tell me this quote. It echoes in my mind! "It's never too late to _____(the right thing)."

Sometimes we think we are too far gone. Maybe the struggle we have been wrestling with has won too many times and we feel like, "why keep fighting?" That temptation never seems to go away. The enemy tries to convince us we will never get to a place of healing and hope. He chides us with guilt and shame. In total contrast, God the Grace-Giver, always gives understanding and hope. Motivating us with His unconditional love, He whispers to us to keep going, keep fighting, keep praying...For He knows doing the right thing will bless us. It is never too late!

What issue do I want to give up on?

God, empower me with YOUR great love. Help me to remember You are always for us, it is never too late. Help me to focus on Your truth and give me strength to overcome struggles in my life. In Jesus name

Who can I give life to today?

DAY 73

Great things in my life:

1.
2.
3.
4.
5.

"The Lord makes firm the steps of the one who delights in Him; though he may stumble, he will not fall, for the Lord upholds him with His hand." (Psalms 37:23- 24 NIV)

What does it mean to "delight" in the Lord? This is not a theological answer. To me, "delight" means to be excited about Him and what He is doing around us. God is always up to something amazing in our life and the lives of the people around us. There will always be the negative or worrisome moments, but we don't have to dwell on those. We can acknowledge those negatives, pray about them, entrust them in God's care, and keep our mind and heart focused on the delightful!

What good things are happening in my life?

What good things are happening in the lives of the people around me?

God, thank You for the good stuff (the delightful) that You are doing in my life and the lives of those around me. In Jesus name

Who can I give life to today?

I am thankful for:

1.
2.
3.
4.
5.

"On your feet now—applaud God!
Bring a gift of laughter,
sing yourselves into his presence.
Know this: God is God, and God, God.
He made us; we didn't make him.
We're his people, his well-tended sheep.
Enter with the password: "Thank you!"
Make yourselves at him, talking praise.
Thank him. Worship him.
For God is sheer beauty,
all-generous in love,
loyal always and ever." *(Psalms 100 MSG)*

"Bring a gift of laughter!" Do I think about God loving to hear me laugh? He does! God gives us the gift of fun, adventure, and laughter!"

God, I am so thankful for You and Your gift of love.

Who can I give life to today?

What is good in my life?

1.
2.
3.
4.
5.

"None of this fazes us because Jesus loves us. I'm absolutely convinced that nothing—nothing living or dead, angelic or demonic, today or tomorrow, high or low, thinkable or unthinkable—absolutely nothing can get between us and God's love because of the way that Jesus our Master has embraced us." (Romans 8:39 MSG)

What are two things Jesus asks us to do? "Love God, love people."

Because He is the Source of love, I believe there must be a continual stream of love, flowing from His heart to ours, to truly have enough love to give back to Him as well as others around us. His love must fill our hearts, so we can give love back to Him. Life is full of unloving things and disappointments. Yet, God's love is HUGE and nothing can steal it from us. His love is always with us and it doesn't go away when we forget about it.

Do I wrap my thoughts about me in His love daily?

God, make me aware of Your great, never-ending love for me. May there be a continual flow of love from Your heart to mine. In Jesus name

Who can I give life to today?

What do I enjoy?

1.
2.
3.
4.
5.

"But seek (aim at and strive for) first of all His kingdom and His righteousness (His way of doing and being right)..." (Matthew 6:33 AMPC)

When I look at life "His way" from God's perspective, everything looks different. God sees straight to a person's heart—their pain, their insecurities, their whole story. Almost all unkind responses are less about us, and more about what is going on inside of the heart of the person being unkind. When I look at a person's story and can see past their hurtful words or comments, my thoughts about them change, and that changes my interaction with them. When we "strive after" God's way of doing things we love Him first and we love others.

What am I "striving after"?

God, change my perspective. Help me to see life the way You see it. In Jesus name

Who can I give life to today?

DAY 77

I can celebrate:

1.
2.
3.
4.
5.

Celebrating the small and the big leads to excitement!

"This means that anyone who belongs to Christ has become a new person. The old life is gone; a new life has begun!" (2 Corinthians 5:17 NLT)

Do you ever look back at all the photos on your phone? When I do this, I smile, great memories!!! I also ask myself,

- Did I give my best to everyone in whatever situation I was in?
- Was I an encouragement?
- Did I live that moment to the fullest?
- Was I too distracted to listen?
- Did I make the person I was with feel special?

We can look back and live in regret or shame, OR we can look back and think about the good. There is always some good, even if it is a consequence of a negative action we learn from. Then, we can use that as an opportunity to think about how we want to keep improving. We are not defined by our yesterdays, but by God's great love.

Do I think about who I am in God?

God, help me not to live in yesterday or focus on my "I wish I had..." Instead, help me to grow letting Your love define me and from that may I live the life You have for me. In Jesus name

Who can I give life to today?

I am thankful for:

1.
2.
3.
4.
5.

"To "Live freely," don't we all want that?" animated and motivated by God's Spirit. Then you won't feed the compulsions of selfishness." *(Galatians 5:16-17 MSG)*

Live freely- don't we all want that? It is hard to feel free or motivated when there is a negative swirl in our minds. One thing that can rob us from living freely is when someone hurts our feelings and we replay it repeatedly. Most of us do this without realizing it. We say we are fine or we don't care, but inside we keep thinking about the words that were said. This morning, I was doing this and God whispered, "Thinking about this will not bring joy, happiness, or a great day."

Immediately, we can change our thoughts, but if we don't deal with the thought or hurt it will come back.

To get rid of nagging hurtful thoughts, we can:

1. Acknowledge (this person's words bothered me)
2. Choose to forgive them (saying a prayer about this is most powerful)
3. Maybe confront them (this depends on the situation)
4. Stop thinking about it (every time the hurt is replayed, think about something life-giving.)
5. Remind ourselves we already forgave the person

Is something someone did or said bothering you?
Can you choose to deal with this thought?
Life to the full is available to all of us!

God, I can't stop thinking about _____. I give this thought to You, I choose to forgive _____. Please forgive my bitterness toward them. I don't want to let this thought have any power over me, so I give it to You. In Jesus name

Who can I give life to today?

I am thankful for:

1.
2.
3.
4.
5.

"Look at me. I stand at the door. I knock. If you hear me call and open the door, I'll come right in and sit down to supper with you. Conquerors will sit alongside me at the head table, just as I, having conquered, took the place of honor at the side of my Father. That's my gift to the conquerors!" (Revelation 3:20 MSG)

God is always pursuing us, knocking on the door of our lives. He is waiting to be invited into our thoughts, our memories, our pain, our struggles, our relationships, our everyday routine, our future, our dreams...We get to open the door to Him and invite Him into these things. He is always ready to help, often He just wants to be asked. A simple prayer of surrender can do this.

We need to walk with Jesus to live for Jesus. The word Christianity is made up of Christ. Without living in a relationship with Him, we are just living "ianity," which means "emptiness and "shallow." We need a daily walk with Jesus to live the Christian life, it is impossible to be kind and loving without Him. We need Him to be our best self. To give love, we need the source of love to fill us.

When invited, He will empower us.

Does anything hold me back from inviting God into every aspect of my life?

God, I invite YOU to do life with me. In Jesus name

Who can I give life to today?

Who has blessed me?

1.
2.
3.
4.
5.

If we stop for a second and think about 5 people that have helped us or blessed us, we feel gratitude. This gratitude can lead us to help others. God wants us to be so full of His love for us that it spills out on others.

In his book, Everybody Always, Bob Goff has some amazing thoughts on how to love people, "God's endgame has always been the same. He wants our hearts to be His. He wants us to love the people near us and the love the people we've kept far away. To do this, He wants us to live without fear. We don't need to use our opinions or mask our insecurities anymore. Instead, God wants us to grow love in our hearts and cultivate it." (pg. 4 Everybody Always)

Today, may we let go of our own stuff (worries, insecurities, fears) and reach out to someone else. People around us need to see Jesus through us.

Who is one person who I can make their day better today?

God, Help me to stop the negative thoughts about myself and live letting Your love define me. Show me who You want me to reach out to today. In Jesus name

Who can I give life to today?

DAY 81

Good things in my life:

1.
2.
3.
4.
5.

"Since God assured us, "I'll never let you down, never walk off and leave you," we can boldly quote, God is there, ready to help; I'm fearless no matter what. Who or what can get to me?" *(Hebrews 13:5-6 MSG)*

God will never leave us. In this world people let us down sometimes, they reject us, ignore us, or leave us. Without realizing it, subconsciously, we can put human attributes on God. Maybe we think if we do something or don't do something He will get frustrated and give up on us. The enemy tries to convince us of this.

Do I put human attributes on God? (Do I think He will leave? Or reject me? Do I think He gets tired of me and my struggles?)

"Deep within all of us is a longing to love and to be loved, to know that someone cares and will never leave or forsake us. Unfortunately, some people spend a lifetime searching for that kind of love that seems forever beyond reach." (Henri Nouwen)

Thankfully, God in His GREAT tender powerful love is always pursuing us, waiting with us, walking beside us, empowering us, and wrapping us in His love. We can see this through the life of Jesus.

God, thank You that You will never leave me. I invite YOU to live my moments with me filling my heart with Your unconditional healing tender powerful love. In Jesus name

Who can I give life to today?

DAY 82

What is good in my life?

1.

2.

3.

4.

5.

"Are you tired? Worn out? Burned out on religion? Come to me. Get away with me and you'll recover your life. I'll show you how to take a real rest. Walk with me and work with me—watch how I do it. Learn the unforced rhythms of grace. I won't lay anything heavy or ill-fitting on you. Keep company with me and you'll learn to live freely and lightly." *(Matthew 11:28-30 MSG)*

Sometimes I get "tired, worn out, burned out..." Don't you? The rest part of this line says "on religion." When I get burned out it is usually on religion not a relationship. Religion is about rules, stress, people pleasing...In contrast, a relationship with Jesus is life-giving!

God is not stressful or tiring, life is. When we are tired or burned out, we need to figure out why.

To recover God gives us the solution, "walk with me and work with me." What does that look like practically? When we walk with God, we invite Him into our routine and our moments. Throughout the day, when we are discouraged or overwhelmed, we can consciously turn our thoughts to what God says. We live in a world of distraction, so this might look like putting a phrase or verse on our screen saver. Or it might mean setting a phone reminder throughout the day. God can seem very far away in our day to day stuff—however, if we imagine Him walking beside us all day long, we can continually hand Him our stuff. He doesn't get tired of carrying it.

God, walk with me, here are the things that feel overwhelming and stressful (my repetitive worry) _____.
These things are making me feel "burned out" instead I want to feel full of LIFE. Remind me that You are key in this and fill me with Your love as my identity. In Jesus name

Who can I give life to today?

A few GIFTS in my life are:

1.
2.
3.
4.
5.

"So, my very dear friends, don't get thrown off course. Every desirable and beneficial gift comes out of heaven. The gifts are rivers of light cascading down from the Father of Light..." (James 1:17 MSG)

Every gift is from God. When we look around we can thank God for the gifts in our lives.

"Don't get thrown off course," this is the advice in this verse. When we take our focus off of seeing God as the God Who gives good gifts, we wonder if He is good. When we focus on all the negative and forget about our gifts, we get "off course." Because our minds are powerful, they can lead our emotions, feelings and habits, which directs our actions.

Thankfully, it is so easy to get back on course. We can give God our pain or negativity and ask Him to heal the broken places. We can continually remember the good gifts in our life, which leads to us knowing God is good.

Has anything thrown me off course (in my thinking and actions)?

God, thank YOU for loving me and thank you for EVERY single gift. In Jesus name

Who can I give life to today?

DAY 84

What GIFTS has God given me?

1.
2.
3.
4.
5.

"and they shall call His name 'Immanuel'—which, when translated, means, 'God with us.'" (Matthew 1:23 AMP)

When we see God as the Giver of all good things, we are continually thankful. Our perception of God affects everything in life. When we know God is good, we want Him with us. His name reminds us of this.

"God is always near us. Always for us. Always in us. We may forget Him, but God will never forget us. We are forever on His mind and in His plans. He called Himself, "Immanuel' (which means, 'God with us')" (Matt. 1:23).
'God made us.'
Not just, 'God thinks of us.'

Not just, 'God above us.'
But God *with* us.'" (An Angel's Story, Max Lucado)

God with us.

Today, what do I need God to walk beside me in?

God, thank You that You are always with me, always for me, always loving me. May this truth give me strength today. In Jesus name

Who can I give life to today?

What messages are life-giving?

1.
2.
3.
4.
5.

My seventeen year old son, Owin, and I went to Costco yesterday. On accident, we chose the broken cart. Throughout the store, I kept thinking we would get used to the squeaky sound of the wheels, but after shopping for twenty minutes the noise was even more maddening. He decided the only way to fix the problem was getting a new cart, but our cart was full. Because emptying our current cart felt like a huge effort, we kept shopping, probably annoying all of the shoppers around us.

We listen to the same negative message in our brain. Many times it is maddening. Sometimes, we grow accustomed to the annoying noise.

What is a negative message you replay?

Most of us have at least one message that defeats us and makes life less enjoyable.

However, we do have a choice. We don't have to replay the nagging messages, just like Owin and I didn't have to keep the cart we had, we could have gotten a new cart.

Changing thoughts is pretty simple:

1. Identify the one repetitive, negative thought
2. Replace it with a life-giving thought

"We can stop the self-defeating noise in our brain by choosing to think about what God says about us. He says that we are 'for we are God's masterpiece.'" (Ephesians 2:10 NLT)

We aren't stuck, we can get a new, life-giving, repetitive thought.

God, show me what I think that brings me down. When I think this thought, help me remember that I am Your masterpiece. In Jesus name.

Who can I give life to today?

What is good in my life?

1.
2.
3.
4.
5.

"Now we look inside, and what we see is that anyone united with the Messiah gets a fresh start, is created new. The old life is gone." (2 Corinthians 5:17 MSG)

Tuesdays are the day our trash is emptied. By Tuesday our outside garbage cans are usually flowing over and sometimes they stink. Wonderfully, all that disgusting trash is emptied and taken away—forever! As soon as it is emptied we have new stuff to fill it with (getting our mess out of the house).

We live in a world where we are constantly dealing with yuck. People hurt us, we get rejected, we fail. Others around us are hurting. Our struggles and thoughts feel overwhelming, but everyday we get a fresh start, "the old life is gone!" This is

GREAT news. Everyday, we get to give God all of the mess we are dealing with—our pain, our anxiety, our sadness, our sin. He takes it away, just like my Tuesday garbage service.

However, life is hard, so we need Him to take our mess away everyday. When we give Him our mess, we can live life to the fullest. We don't have to worry and our mind is freed to think about the amazing!

What is messy in my life? Do I daily give God all of my junk?

Simple daily prayer:

God, I give You _____ (my struggle, my pain, my anxieties, my fears, my rejection, my loneliness, my anger, my disappointment) please take all of this mess and instead give me Your peace, hope, and joy. Remind me that every moment is a "fresh start." In Jesus name

Who can I give life to today?

DAY 87

I am thankful for:

1.
2.
3.
4.
5.

"The LORD is close to the brokenhearted; he rescues those whose spirits are crushed." (Psalms 34:18 NLT)

On a walk one day I saw a wheel barrow with a sign on it that said, "Free. Needs new tire." It's useless without the tire working, but it is not that hard to fix.

The sign reminded me of a story:

> My blue eyed blond headed three-year old girl rides her bike with reckless abandon racing everywhere. One day, she was peddling slower than normal, I asked her if anything was wrong. She replied, "I can not pedal verwy well." Sure

enough, she had a flat tire. I told her that she would have to get off the bike and dad would fix it when he got home. "No mommy, I can do it." Pedaling got harder and harder, she tried until she was worn out. Getting off the bike, she waited until her dad got home. As he pulled into the driveway, she had the bike ready for him to fix. We do that in life, don't we? We ride along aware that something is lopsided, knowing something is not right. We make excuses and pedal harder with a keen sense that there is a broken place that needs repair. God gently nudges us, but we pedal on harder, faster and we do not get very far. We peddle on in life until we crash or get so tired we just cannot go on like this anymore. (The Treasure)

Because life is full of uncertainty, we constantly face things that could hurt our hearts. Yet, God fixes the pain in our heart, even if the circumstance does not always change. We need Him, the Good Father to restore us, so we can keep walking the life He has for us.

Is there anything that makes me feel worn out like I am pedaling on flats?

God, here is my heart, my mind, my emotions, my situations, I invite Jesus in to heal me. I need You to fix the broken places, so that I can life to the FULLEST. In Jesus name

Who can I give life to today?

What is great in my life?

1.
2.
3.
4.
5.

"We pray that you'll have the strength to stick it out over the long haul—not the grim strength of gritting your teeth but the glory-strength God gives. It is the strength that endures the unendurable and spills over into joy, thanking the Father who makes us strong enough to take part in everything bright and beautiful that he has for us." (Colossians 1:11-12 MSG)

Spills...growing up with four siblings, we spilled at least once a meal and my dad would always laugh and say, "well, now that that's over, we can enjoy our meal." His comment took the stress off and made us all laugh. My first job as a 16-year-old was working at Sonic when they still had roller skating servers. My first week on the job, I skated out to a beautiful, brand new, shiny red Porsche and delivered four of our largest drinks. Needless to say, I spilled all of them on the car that belonged to the owner. He didn't laugh.

Accidental spills and little mess ups happen. What do we do after we spill? So much of life comes down to our responses. I am so thankful my dad taught me to laugh at spills—it's made my own home a lot less stressful.

There are two things we can ask ourselves:

- How do I respond when I spill? (or make a mistake)
- How do I respond when others around me spill on me?

We get to choose our response and the way we handle life's messes, we can choose joy and wisdom or, we can choose to overreact. No one is going to remember the spill we made, but people will remember our response. Life is full of the unexpected and can be messy at times. We get to choose our thoughts, which lead to our reactions. Choosing laughter is much better than crying or getting mad.

God, if I saw the big picture like You do, I believe I would take life a lot less seriously, laughing more often and forgiving myself and others more freely. Help me to see life through Your eyes. In Jesus name

Who can I give life to today?

DAY 89

What makes me smile?

1.
2.
3.
4.
5.
6.
7.

"Give thanks in ALL circumstances..." (1 Thessalonians 5:18)

We are given hundreds of gifts each day. Each moment is a GIFT. We get to choose to embrace every moment and live life to the fullest! We can look back and wish for do-overs, or we can learn from regret and live giving life.

Am I living moments enjoying life?

It is almost impossible to thrive around negativity or frustration, instead we can be constant life-givers. Living to GIVE fills us with inner joy. May we savor every moment living out the joy that God placed in us and give His love to others.

God, help me to give life to others. Help me to live hopeful and joyful so that I enjoy the life You have given me. In Jesus name

Who can I give life to today?

What can I celebrate? (working hard, a great moment, doing something out of my comfort zone..)

1.
2.
3.

"Celebrate God all day, every day." (Philippians 4:4 MSG)

We forget to CELEBRATE!

Please take a moment and thank God for all the good around you. When we do this, we feel better. We celebrate God's goodness in our life.

Next, you can remind yourself of something you have done that was hard or lonely or uncomfortable or out of your comfort zone-and celebrate progress!

How can you celebrate? (Example: take an hour to do something you love or hang out with a friend..) You get to choose your celebration!

Most of us are very aware of all of the things we miss or where we mess up. Because of this, we can forget to celebrate great moments.

God, I celebrate Your blessings in my life and I celebrate the good! In Jesus name

LIFE TO THE FULLEST

Living a routine of Choosing Life to the Fullest might take more than 90 days. (Book 1 and 2 provide 180 days)

Routines take time, if you enjoyed this book, you can go through it again or keep this routine going by:

1. Starting everyday thinking: "What 5 things am I thankful for?"
2. Whisper a prayer: "God, thank you for these things, and Jesus, I invite You into my day, my heart, my life, my words, my thoughts... In Your name"
3. Throughout the day, identify every self-defeating thought and change it to a GREAT one. (You can do this by choosing a verse, quote, or song to replay in your mind.) This is simple, but life-changing.
4. Repeatedly think, "God is for me. He loves me, because He made me. As I embrace the love of Jesus, my life will radically change."
5. Set a reminder to do something small to bless someone every day.

NOTES

Goff, B. (2017). *Everybody always.* Tommy Nelson

Leaf, C. (2017). *Switch on your brain.* Baker Books

Newberry, T. (2012). *40 days to a joy-filled life.* Carol Stream, IL: Tyndale House.

Gunyon, B. (2018). *The Treasure. living immersed in His love.* Westbow: A Division of Tommy Nelson and Zondervan

Henderson, J. (2019). *Know What You're FOR.* Zondervan

Larson, S. (2016) *Your powerful prayers.* Bethany House Publishers

Lucado, Max. (2002) *An angel's story.* W Publishing Group a division of Tommy Nelson Publishing

Amplified Bible (AMPC). The Lockman Foundation, 1954, 1958, 1962, 1964, 1965, 1987

The Christian Standard Bible. Holman Bible Publishers. 2017

Easy To Read Version; Bible League international, 2006

God's Word. God's Word to the Nations. 1995

Good News Translation (Today's English Version, Second Edition). 1992 American Bible Society.

Holy Bible, New Living Translation, 1996, 2004, 2015 by Tyndale House Foundation. Used by permission of Tyndale House Publishers, Inc., Carol Stream, Illinois 60188.

NET Bible. Biblical Studies Press, L.L.C., 1996-2006

New Century Version. Thomas Nelson. 2005

New American Standard Bible. Copyright by The Lockman Foundation 1960, 1962, 1963, 1968, 1971, 1972, 1973, 1975, 1977, 1995

International Children's Bible. Thomas Nelson, Inc., 1986, 1988, 1999, 2015

The Holy Bible: English Standard Version. Crossway, a publishing ministry of Good News Publishers, 2016

The Holy Bible: New International Version. Biblica, Inc., 1973, 1978, 1984, 2011

Peterson, Eugene H. The Message Tyndale House Publishers, Inc., 1993, 2002, 201

The Bible in Worldwide English. Educational Publications, Derby DE65 6BN, UK.

NOTE FROM THE AUTHOR

"Amid my search for significance and approval, God whispered to me on a mountain in Colorado. While serving on summer staff at Frontier Ranch, a Young Life Camp, His still small voice spoke to my heart and said, "You are loved by Me. Really loved by Me - not because of what you do- but because I love you. I, Jesus, absolutely love you." (*The Treasure*) Twenty-four years ago, He whispered this message that forever changed my life.

The love of Jesus consumed my heart and continues to fill it with a love so big. This Love became my passion - to share the heart of God. My hope and prayer is that others will embrace the love of Jesus and let it transform their thoughts. It took years to undo the destructive negative thoughts that I lived immersed in. The eating disorder that I struggled with from age ten to twenty-one wreaked havoc on my identity and the way I thought God saw me. Yet, when the love of God captured my heart, my thoughts started to change. I began to "live life to the fullest."

After nineteen years of mentoring and counseling teens at The Way Counseling, I am convinced teens are continually battling their thoughts - we can think ourselves into greatness or destruction.

This book began as a short daily thoughts devotion for my own three teens. I decided to post it on @chooselifetothefullest. My kids' friends started reading. After a few weeks, I found myself teary, my own kids told me they were reading and I could see their countenance changing- they acted more positive, more hopeful, and full of joy. My seventeen-year old, who plays very competitive baseball, started laughing and letting go of the stress. My sixteen-year old daughter started giving me wise advice about what God was showing her. My fourteen-year old was grumpy with me one day said, "Mom, I just didn't start off the day thinking great." They are all understanding the importance of thinking great and living inviting Jesus in. It is my hope that all who read will discover how powerful this is!

Reading book one and two will provide 180 days of thinking great and inviting Jesus in, this can become a habit that changes a life forever! This is my hope, that in thinking great and inviting Jesus into your thoughts that you will truly live life to the FULLEST!